£2-00

# PORT AFTER STORMY SEAS
# A SAILOR'S TALE

## A. E. Garrod

**MINERVA PRESS**
WASHINGTON LONDON MONTREUX

**PORT AFTER STORMY SEAS – A SAILOR'S TALE**
Copyright © A. E. Garrod 1996

ISBN 1 85863 912 3

First Published 1996 by
MINERVA PRESS
195 Knightsbridge,
London SW7 1RE

Printed in Great Britain
B.W.D. Ltd., Northolt, Middlesex

# PORT AFTER STORMY SEAS

## A SAILOR'S TALE

*The author presented with the Malta Commemorate Medal at Palace Valletta by the President of Malta, Dr Censu Tabone, Wednesday 19th May, 1993.*

*This book is dedicated to:*

*My wife, Irene, for her patience, and encouragement!*

*Sons, Alan, and Neil, for having 'given birth' to the original idea!*

*Celia Evans, for her unstinting, untiring support!*

*Doctor W.J.C. Roberts, of Aberystwyth, whose medical skills, and caring, compassionate approach, enabled me to carry on, when the darkness of the past, threatened to overshadow the happiness of the present!*

*All ex-shipmates, wherever they may be, for having helped to make the 'unbearable', bearable!*

*A.E. Garrod*
*October, 1994*
*Trepechan, Wales*

Sleep after toil, port after stormy seas.
Ease after war, death after life does greatly please.


Edmund Spenser

(1552-1599)

# PROLOGUE

This is not a book for the fact-seeking historian, for the academic, in search of further enlightenment, or for lovers of the intricacies of 'war games'. It is simply a book to be read, and, hopefully, enjoyed, and as I kept no record of events, as they occurred, an exercise of both memory, and recollection. It was necessary to change the given names of some characters mentioned, in order to avoid embarrassment, both to them, and to their relatives, and I make no apology for doing so!

A.E. GARROD (MR).
APRIL, 1995
ABERYSTWYTH, WALES

# CHAPTER ONE

*Goodmayes, Essex*
*September, 1939.*

The thin, tired voice crackled from the radio in the corner of the room, on to the ears of the family grouped around it. Dad, strict, hardworking, an ex-Navy man. Mum, stout and jolly, who could conjure up a tasty meal from practically nothing, and in spite of the hardship of working-class life in pre-war Britain, and having to raise a large family, managed to present a smiling face and ready ear to anyone in the street who came to her for comfort or solace. Ernest, the eldest son, and myself, Sam, both on leave from the Royal Hospital School, Holbrook, Suffolk, a Naval training school for the sons and grandsons of ex-Navy men, known as the 'Cradle of the Navy'. Three younger sisters completed the group. So it was War! Dad's eyes met mine across the room, and I knew what he was thinking. How long would it last? Would the boys have to go?

Suddenly, the wail of an air raid siren split the still, warm air. Fear hit the stomach like a punch to the solar plexus. We made for the shelter in an orderly fashion, reflecting our naval training. A young female neighbour, whose husband was at work, promptly had hysterics and clutching her small baby to her heaving breast, screamed her way to the garden shelter, flinging herself into it from a distance, badly grazing her knees and elbows in the process. The baby, fortunately, was unharmed. The all-clear soon sounded and we scrambled thankfully from the shelter and headed indoors for a welcome cup of tea.

Ernest and I still had a few weeks of leave left, so we decided to canvass the so-called 'posh' houses which had just been built on the edge of our predominately working-class estate to see if anyone wanted a hole dug in the garden to accommodate an Anderson shelter. Many people had thought that war would not come, so hadn't bothered to install a shelter, but when, to their dismay, war was declared quickly followed by that first 'warning', they couldn't get them in fast enough. The demand was there so we started. We charged £2, hole only, which satisfied the 'customer' and seemed a fortune to us. That summer was hot and dry; we were young and keen and worked like

'Trojans', so the pounds rolled in. Jugs of cool lemonade, platefuls of delicious sandwiches and many other delicacies, provided by our grateful clients, slipped down our ever-hungry throats. We developed muscles on our muscles, a beautiful golden tan, and a liking for money that never left us.

At last our leave was over and it was time to return to the School and reality. Ernest went into the Navy and on 8$^{th}$ May 1940, at the tender age of 15 years, 5 months, I followed him as a Boy Seaman, 2$^{nd}$ Class. I took and passed the entrance exam at *HMS Ganges*, Shotley, just across the river Stour, from Holbrook and left the same day with twenty other lads of similar age for Liverpool, where we spent the night in the Sailors Rest in Paradise Road. My bed that night was a mattress laid on a billiard table and the other lads were similarly accommodated, some on the floor, others on benches scattered around the room. We slept the sleep of the young and the innocent and awoke, next morning, none the worse for it, and prepared to face whatever the day might bring. After a hearty breakfast, we gathered up our few possessions and calling farewell to the kindly people who, in spite of difficulties, had cared for us so well, embussed for the Isle of Man ferry terminal and the crossing, our first spell of 'sea time'.

The journey passed without incident and we disembarked at Douglas, Isle of Man and were transported to Howstrake Camp, a former holiday centre, poised high on rugged cliffs overlooking Douglas and swept continuously (it seemed) by high winds, with the sound of roaring seas forever pounding the jagged rocks far below.

Here we 'suffered' our initial training, which consisted mainly of squad drills with endless marching up and down, with so many changes of direction and raucous, shouted orders that finally our minds became numbed and we had no tangible idea in which direction we were moving, or supposed to be moving. One mindbending chore was the sewing into every item of kit possible of our initials and surname, a time when the advantage of being a SMITH or JONES was much appreciated, and one boy, for the first time, was happy to have been named 'GUY'. However, with sore fingers, blistered feet and a great sense of our utter uselessness and stupidity, which the instructors constantly hammered into our bemused minds, we completed our 'New Entry' course and were deemed ready to face the rigours of life in the Main Camp and the comparative sanity of a

Seaman Boys training course. This consisted of one year's instruction in Gunnery and Seamanship, with a liberal sprinkling of physical training and sport to break the monotony.

We were billeted in chalets, four boys to each, sleeping in two-tiered iron beds. We kept the chalet clean at all times and our personal gear stowed away tidily. We learned to leave nothing lying about for not only would this be a 'bad mark' against the occupants, but also someone would probably pinch it, and all items of kit lost had to be replaced from our meagre pay. Looking back on this period many years afterward, I believe I enjoyed it, fortunate in being one of a class (174 A.C. Class, as we were officially known), of very high standard generally both in character and in intelligence, with a deep sense of 'All for One and One for All', which was a great asset in those difficult days.

Seaman Boys were of two origins. Some were ex-training ship boys (like myself) known as 'Ship' boys. The remainder were from 'civvy', homes, straight from the shelter of loving (or otherwise) parents and some of these boys suffered intensely, at first, from homesickness and a general sense of despair!

At night, they sobbed quietly in their solitary bunk and by day they stumbled awkwardly through a daily routine which seemed to have been deliberately designed to trap the unwary and to bring down the wrath of some bellowing instructor on their hapless head. We 'old' hands noted their suffering and helped them when we could until, eventually, they succeeded in putting their 'old' life behind them, became 'one of the crowd', some of them so completely that they were able to show us a few new tricks.

Each weekday, rain, snow, or blow, we marched, with four drummers at the head, to the school at Ballykameen, a distance of some four-and-a-half miles, crossing on the way the bridge at Santon, known locally as the 'Fairy Bridge', where we were encouraged to say 'Good Morning' to the 'little people', thus ensuring good fortune for the rest of the day. When darkness fell early, the front and rear fours, dressed in long white smocks carried lighted oil lanterns and, to my knowledge, no accidents occurred during these night marches.

Most of the instructors were dedicated and hardworking men, but the occasional sadist reared his ugly head. At that time a story in *The Beano* was very popular with the boys. I believe it was called 'The Wolf of Kabul' and in it the hero 'set about' rebel Afghan tribesmen with a cricket bat, which he called 'Clicky Ba'. Incredibly, one instructor copied the fictional hero and, if a boy upset him during the day, usually by making a mistake on the parade ground, he was detailed off to report to the instructors cabin clad in a pair of sports shorts that evening. The boy was ordered to 'bend over' and then whacked across the bum with 'Clicky Ba'. This may sound amusing to some people but I was assured by one of the victims that it was an extremely painful experience.

My own gunnery instructor was a veritable giant, with a much battered face, souvenir of many an encounter in the boxing ring and many outside it too! He was reputed to have been an ex-heavyweight champion of the China Fleet (we had one, in those days) in his youth and quite frankly, from his appearance, I believed it! He was as tough as he looked, as events proved. One day, during rifle drill, one of the squad broke wind and the smell was appalling! Someone started to titter and soon, as often happens, everyone was convulsed! The instructor was not amused and quickly wanted to know what the joke was? Of course, no one would 'shop' the culprit and the instructor acted swiftly! 'Gas' he bellowed (not inappropriately) and we quickly donned the ever present gas masks slung over our shoulders. 'Slope arms' came the next command followed by 'Double march'. There we were, with fixed bayonets at the slope, wearing gas masks, doubling up and down which as anyone with similar experience knows is well beyond a joke! He halted us and rapped 'Off masks' and again asked who the culprit was. To their eternal credit no one answered and we were mentally preparing for another spell of blistering, choking doubling, when the culprit, Tom Pepper from Gravesend, Kent, stepped forward and we sighed with relief. 'Report to Sick Bay', bellowed the instructor, 'and tell them who sent you'. Tom doubled off smartly and we resumed our drill.

Sometime later, the gallant Tom reappeared and reported to the instructor who asked him what the 'sick bay tiffy' had said. Tom replied, 'That big ugly bastard's a nuisance, he's always sending people down here!' The instructor puffed up with rage, like a rampant bullfrog and ordering a leading boy to take charge, vanished in the direction of the Sick Bay at a rate of knots. We heard, afterwards, that he charged in, a truly terrifying sight, seized the 'tiffy' and lifted him off the ground, threatening to grind him into little pieces if he ever insulted him again. The 'tiffy' was duly impressed!

Bill Leggett's life was his squad and although he gave us a hard time woe betide any 'outsider', officer, or instructor who tried to interfere or make a derogatory remark, about his 'lads'. Competition between classes was fierce in the classroom, on the parade ground and on the sports field, and any boy who showed outstanding talent, particularly at sporting activities, was encouraged to the full to develop that talent with the full weight of the system behind him. Of course when the class did well the instructor reaped his share of the 'glory' as was proper, for after all, he motivated them and guided their efforts in the right direction.

It was decided to award 'colours' in the form of a strip of coloured ribbon, to be sewn on the left breast of the standard sports shirt, to those boys who showed outstanding talent in sporting activities, be it football, cricket, hockey, running, swimming, boxing or even leaping about in the gym. I was always a 'natural' at most sports and before long strode proudly about the camp like a miniature Hermann Goering. Throughout my Service career, I was always involved in sport of some kind and found it the key to many a door which would otherwise have been closed to me. Maybe the fact that I never trained, performed so well and was always in demand, was the reason that success, in the terms of medals or outstanding fame, never came my way. It was too easy and I enjoyed it all, with the exception of cricket, which bored me to tears although I still played. At Holbrook, Commander Lamb, who ran the school cricket team, was most upset when I failed to attend for net practice and I was definitely not his blue-eyed boy after that heinous offence, although I still continued to play well in cricket matches both home and away. Captain Bruce-Gardyne, R.N., however, the school Superintendent, was a keen boxing fan and always picked my face from the crowd when moving around the school and asked detailed questions about my latest fight, which he always attended. For some strange reason, he always called me 'Turtle' and never got my name right and when, once, I dared to question this, he replied intently, 'Your style reminds me of him'. Trouble was no one seemed to know who the mysterious 'Turtle' was and I was much too overawed to question such an 'august' figure too closely.

Tom Pepper (the wind-breaker), an ex-Arethusa boy, was a rough looking lad built like an all-wrestler, with an honest, generous nature, which belied his tough upbringing around the streets of Gravesend, Kent. His parents divorced when he was young and his father, with whom he was very close, tried to obtain a place for him at the Royal Hospital School, Holbrook, but was unsuccessful. He then tried T.S. Arethusal, a Shaftesbury Homes training ship, which was then moored at Upnor, on the river Medway, opposite Chatham Dockyard and this time, was successful. So off Tom duly went, to climb the rigging, pull the boats and to live a life tough enough to make the Navy training, a veritable piece of cake. We joined the Royal Navy together, on the same day, he from Arethusa, myself from R.H.S. We became, in Navy parlance, 'oppo's in a friendship that lasted many years, till fate took a hand and we parted bitter enemies.

Time passed rapidly and we were trained to a hair, fit and ready for anything, and raring to go! One day, I was ordered to report to the divisional office and with some trepidation, off I went. On arrival, the blow fell! In wartime, boys under the age of seventeen years could only go to sea with their parents' written permission. My parents had refused to give that permission which meant that instead of being drafted to a sea-going ship with my 'oppo's, I would have to remain on shore until reaching the required age.

As far as we knew, all the other parents had signed the required forms and I was the only boy in the class who had to remain behind. I was truly devastated and very angry and wrote my parents a bitter diatribe against them and their decision. I threatened never to see them again and, at the time, really meant every word. Anyway, it worked, for shortly afterwards, I was informed that all was now well and I could proceed to sea with the rest of the lads. We were then around sixteen and a half years old.

The final six weeks were spent in 'Land Fighting', which was intended to prepare us for fighting ashore, usually in support of the Army, such as in the Dardennelles action, in World War One and the many shore activities by the Navy, i.e. beach parties at invasion points etc. in World War Two. We dressed in well-scrubbed 'duck suits', with gaiters, webbing and backpacks and carried out fast marches over many kinds of terrain, rehearsing the field signals and manoeuvres employed when facing an enemy force. Occasionally, when on a march, we encountered a mass of 18b detainees who were imprisoned in large numbers in the I.O.M. many in former hotels situated along the seafront at Douglas, supposedly to prevent them from passing information which might be useful to the enemy. Whatever the rights, or wrongs, of that political decision, they looked a sad and shabby group, shuffling along, with heads low, a look of utter misery in their haunted eyes. They must have thought 'Christ, the British are robbing the cradle too', but we didn't care what they thought, as long as they were suitably impressed!

End of course examinations next. Back to the parade ground again. Marching, counter-marching, shouted commands, but no insults this time. We and the instructors knew our work and each other too well. Written exams, seamanship and gunnery, with growing confidence and sense of pride in achievement. Boat pulling in Douglas harbour, remembered chiefly by the event of a dirty great seagull, shitting a 'clump block', which landed on the knife-edge crease of my immaculate white shorts, thereby ruining my day completely!

Finally, dinner at the Villa Marina, Douglas, for the boxing team of which I was a member. C.P.O. Bill Leggett, who had left the I.O.M. before completion of the course on promotion to Warrant Officer, which in our opinion he richly deserved, was the unanimous choice of the boys as guest of honour and that veteran of many a bruising encounter in the boxing ring sat there, beaming with pride and happiness, on what was, for everyone present, a most enjoyable evening and a truly memorable occasion.

We spent a year in the Isle of Man and I remember, to this day, the exceptional warmth and kindness of the Manx people. They could easily have looked upon us as intruders and have treated us accordingly, but they took us to their hearts and helped, in many ways, to make our comfortless lives more bearable. Free trips to the cinema were arranged, huge bags of chips could be cheaply purchased, very important where hungry young boys were concerned and a friendly smile or a kindly word were exchanged whenever our paths crossed.

Time to leave *HMS St. George* and the Isle of Man and begin the long journey by boat, train and lorry to another 'stone frigate', *HMS Pembroke*, Chatham, Kent, there to await a 'draft chit' to a sea-going ship, we fervently hoped, and a chance to put into action some of the training at which we had worked so hard and for so long.

# CHAPTER TWO

*HMS Pembroke*
*May, 1941.*

A shock awaited us! The barracks were full to overflowing and the special messing facilities required for boy sailors were not available. Some three miles away, at Borstal, near Rochester, Kent, stood the establishment for young offenders under the age of twenty-one known as the Borstal Institute. There, youngsters who had fallen foul of the law were subjected to strict discipline under prison like conditions and taught a trade in order to 'rehabilitate' them, thus enabling them to become useful and law-abiding members of society. At least that was the theory, but in practice, many learned the tricks of the villain's trade and came out bigger crooks than when they went inside. Still, I suppose the authorities had a measure of success and I know that the Americans sent several fact finding missions to examine and evaluate the system. Borstal was to be our new 'home'.

A wall across the yard, inside the entrance block, divided us from the 'other prisoners' and we soon settled in, two to a cell, in bunk beds. We were next kitted out in the usual Service style. Bell bottomed jumpers and skin-tight trousers. Nothing was expected to fit anyway! That was the system! The final indignity was that the clothing store was manned by WRNS, who flung the gear at us with all the aplomb of seasoned 'Jack Dusty' and with the same command (or lack of it) of the English language. I formed an instant dislike of WRNS in general and that dislike was fanned by the preferential treatment they were accorded at all times, by reason of their sex, which they exploited to the full.

Life settled into an easy pattern after the stresses and strains of training at 'St George'. I first worked in the dining hall, operating a washing-up machine after meals with little else to do except to sit around yarning, or to drift from cell to cell, to wherever the most interesting 'action' took place. We were not allowed leave, hence the 'other prisoners' term, used earlier. My second favourite 'hobby', reading, proved as always, a great boon.

Soon, I was detailed off for aircraft lookout duties, which, at the least, provided some wonderful views of the local countryside. The main entrance to the Institute, was a massive, square, fortress-like building, which housed the offices and administrative department and, having a flat roof, provided an ideal post for an all-round view of the sprawling buildings and playing fields of the establishment. Armed with a pair of powerful binoculars and a massive sense of responsibility, I prowled my domain, protecting the lives and well-being of my comrades far below. The idea was that on receipt of a 'red warning' over the field telephone, thoughtfully provided, the 'lookout' would hoist a red flag at the masthead on the roof and, with the 'glasses', watch for any aircraft making a definite attack on the Borstal complex. Such attacks would be reported over the telephone, an alarm sounded and everyone would make for the shelters. How practical the scheme would proved to have been we never found out, for the German aircraft showed a singular lack of interest in our activities, so the sun shone, the birds sang and time passed quite happily in our isolated 'prison'.

On the 'other side' of the dividing wall was the farm, completely enclosed by a high wall, where the inmates worked during the day growing vegetables, which helped to make the place self-supporting and taught the lads the rudiments of farming. Outside in the surrounding fields, with their outbuildings, cowsheds, etc., pigs and cows roamed munching the lush, green grass and providing milk, butter, cheese and, of course, meat to feed the ever-hungry bellies of those confined within the high walls. We received our 'tickler' ration, the famous tins of cigarette tobacco, the contents of which, we rolled into 'smokes', or used to barter for other goods. We lookouts, when on watch, helped pass the time by rolling cigarettes and when the Borstal boys came near the wall, which they soon learned to do, dropped them batches of cigarettes which they acknowledged with a cheery wave and went on their way rejoicing! Outside and in front of the forbidding entrance block, fine lawns were laid out, edged with colourful flower beds, in which roses, in a veritable multitude of varieties and colours, filled the air with their fragrance providing a delicate contrast to the earthy odours emanating from the nearby farm buildings. Those fine gardens played a bitter role in a later episode of this story.

Came the great day when news of leave, at last, filled the air and dominated our waking thoughts and conversations. 'Foreign Service Draft Leave', were the magic words and we were suddenly uplifted, excited and impatient to be away, sailing the oceans of the world, smiting the enemies of our beloved country and putting to good use the experience gained from our long, expensive training.

Fourteen days' leave for all fifty Naval boys in the establishment. The place buzzed with excitement! 'Tiddley' suits were pressed, shoes were mirror polished and 'old sweats', light blue collars prepared. Potential attacking aircraft became of very minor importance, daily chores quite enjoyable and high walls 'disappeared', in the feverish excitement of leave fever. Ration books and leave passes were issued and in a laughing, chattering, blue-clad throng we skipped to the waiting buses taking us to Chatham Railway Station and the start of our journey home.

Mum and Dad, their family reduced in number from seven to two, the girls having been evacuated to Wiltshire, had moved to a smaller house in Dagenham and quickly slotted into the new community. Dad helped produce munitions at Woolwich Arsenal and fire-watched at night, whilst Mum kept house and readily lent a plump, kindly shoulder to any neighbour who needed one to cry or lean on.

Dad had painted the inside of the Anderson shelter in the garden, fitted it with comfortable bunk beds, lighting and small stove to 'brew up' on and to provide warmth on cold, winter nights. He and Mum had decided to make the best of a bad situation and to make life as comfortable as was possible, so they evolved a routine of preparing for bed early, before the almost predictable, arrival of the bombers and after locking the house, retired to the relative security of the shelter and its creature comforts. That way, when Dad wasn't fire-watching, they at least had a comfortable night's sleep in comparative safety.

I stayed at the 'new' house during my leave and the full horror of the 'Blitz' impressed itself upon me! Death rained from the skies nightly, aerial torpedoes, massive bombs, indiscriminately scattered carpets of incendiaries and the deceptively gently, swaying parachute mine, devastated whole rows of houses and killed or maimed those unfortunates who happened to be inside or nearby.

Many were the unsung heroes of this time, whose only reward, was the satisfaction of having risked their lives to save others and to have seen the joy and the happiness of those whose loved ones were restored to them alive after having been buried in a mountain of rubble, or been rescued from the height of a burning building.

One night, after an evening on the 'juice' in Barking, some three miles distance, I decided to walk home and enjoy the night air. All was well, until passing the local cemetery, which was surrounded by a high, iron, railing fence. I happened to glance left into the cemetery and saw something which, in my inebriated state, looked tall, white and was following me. The faster I walked, the faster it went, until I was moving at a rate of knots. My heart raced, temples throbbed and hairs on the back of my neck stood like hedgehog spines. Suddenly, a loud, raucous voice shouted, 'Halt, who goes there?' I was a shaking, quivering heap! Fortunately, I answered something reassuring to the owner of the voice and a 'pongo' came forward carefully, with rifle at the ready and wanted to know what I was doing wandering about at that time of night. When he saw a solitary matelot, he became quite friendly and we stood chatting for a while. Apparently, the Home Guard had established a check point in the centre of a grassed round-about in front of the Thatched House pub (conveniently) and with the current parachutist scare were checking everything that moved. We walked back apace to the cemetery and observed together that when moving past the railings, the white statues inside seemed to be moving too! A much shaken and nearly sober, matelot finished the walk home much relieved. Thank God for the Home Guard!

On the last Sunday, with just four days' leave left, we decided that a family visit to my grandmother was in order. She lived in Romford, a bus ride away, with Dad's brother George, so off we went to the nearest bus stop (very few working-class people had cars then) and after an uneventful journey, enjoyed a casual happy, family day. We left at about four o'clock and caught the next bus home, but on walking down the street to our house it was soon obvious that something was afoot. Neighbours were at their front door and one came over to Dad, saying that a policeman had been around several times asking if anyone knew where we were but wouldn't leave a message, saying that he would be back later. Everyone in the street had someone serving in the forces, husband, brother, boyfriend, son or relative of some kind and a visit by a policeman in wartime usually meant bad news. Shaken, we trooped indoors, a dark shadow of fear hanging over us. Brother, Ernest, was serving in *HMS Sussex*, a County class cruiser, at that time and our first thoughts were of him and his well-being or otherwise. After a welcome cup of tea, we settled down to await the policeman's return, with much trepidation.

Some hours later, came a loud knocking at the front door. Dad opened it and there stood a large policeman, notebook in hand.

'For you, Sam,' said Dad and, knees shaking, forward I went.

'Are you Sam Garrod, C/JX 194787?' the policeman said sternly.

'Yes, sir,' said I, somewhat shakily.

'You are ordered back to your ship, by noon tomorrow. Is that understood?' he said firmly.

'Yes, officer,' I replied, heart dropping swiftly to the region of my shoes and then settling somewhere around the stomach area.

'Thank you, sir,' said the policeman and walked off importantly down the path, leaving behind a household, thankful that our worst fears were unfounded, but shattered at this finale to what had been a happy day. Next morning, I rose early and after dressing, prepared to face what was for me the ordeal of tackling one of Mum's formidable breakfasts, for which she was justly famous!

Normally, I never ate at that hour, preferring a cup of tea and a 'fag', but Mum's idea seemed to be to cram sufficient food into me in order to sustain me 'till next we meet'! Anyway, I managed to 'perform' to her satisfaction and then, gathering together my few possessions, prepared to leave.

Although I was then but sixteen years old, my life till then had been just one series of goodbyes. Holbrook at twelve years of age meant three years of goodbyes after seasonal home leave, then another year at Douglas, Isle of Man, meant even more farewells, so I was no stranger to them. To be perfectly honest, I can't remember one significant incident in all those farewells, both till then, and in the years to follow. In fact, the times when my sons, Alan and Neil, have left for far-off climes, have caused me far more anguish and are much more vivid in my memory. Bus to Dagenham Station, train to Tilbury Ferry Terminal, ferry across the river Thames to Gravesend. Bus to Chatham, but this time jumping off at Star Hill, Rochester, for the bus to Cookham Wood, for the Borstal Institute and back to the ever open arms of the Duty PO, whose friendly greeting was, 'Where have you been, the others were back hours ago?' Oh well, it's good to be missed!

After settling in, we found that only twenty of the original fifty boys had been recalled and those had been selected on the basis of living nearest the Institute. No-one could, or would say why we had been recalled and had lost four of our precious days' leave. With the traditional British obsession with secrecy went the usual Navy reluctance to tell the ratings anything, unless the ship was sinking, then they grudgingly piped, 'Abandon Ship'.

Life quickly returned to 'normal' and I soon made the acquaintance of those fine lawns at the front of the buildings that I mentioned earlier, being detailed off to spend the hot, sunny days walking in front of a big petrol mower making sure that no large stones in the grass damaged precious blades. That's how I was 'gainfully employed' for four mind boggling days, until the unhappy faces of the remainder of the boys hove into view, having completed their leave. Another Service 'balls up', just one of many, which sowed the seeds of an anti-service feeling, which eventually, led to so many highly skilled, highly trained men leaving the Navy at the first available opportunity.

Liverpool again, after yet another long journey, by lorry and train, humping the inevitable kitbag and hammock, drinking the usual grotty tea and arriving tired, dirty and hungry, back at the by now familiar Sailors Rest in Paradise Road.

Not a Liverpool of old though, but a rather battered city, reeking of woodsmoke, with ruined buildings everywhere, but still alive with the cheeky, chirpy, indomitable spirit of the 'Scousers' shining through. The Luftwaffe had paid the city many visits in an attempt to break the spirit of the people and to reduce the steady flow of vital shipping using the docks. They failed on both counts. 'Scousers' were used to hard times, anyway, so they shrugged their shoulders, uttered some unprintable but succinct comment and carried on doing what had to be done.

That night, at the Sailors Rest, an E.N.S.A. show was the main attraction and we entered into the spirit of the occasion with great gusto! A female singer, requiring a partner for a duet rendering of a popular song of that time, 'Little Sir Echo', delighted us when she dragged on stage our biggest boy, over six feet tall and with a voice like a foghorn. In every group of boys there always seems to be one lad, bigger and stronger than his fellows, who can be a force for good or evil within that group. The good influence is usually a genial giant, the good-humoured butt of many a well-meant joke, with good temper and a mellow disposition.

The evil influence is basically a bully, who uses his extra size and strength to terrorise his smaller and weaker contemporaries. Bill

Houghton fell into the latter category. He once attempted to beat me to a pulp for daring to suggest that German bombers would ever succeed in dropping bombs on London, a suggestion which he considered unpatriotic, but in the aftermath of Rotterdam, Warsaw, etc., I considered quite feasible. His cruel lips curled, his piggy eyes blazed and his huge fists pummelled away at my tough, smaller body, until he tired of it and looked around for a softer, easier target.

He bullied those he considered his inferiors, but 'sucked up' in a sickening fashion to the instructors or any officer within reach. Overall, a nasty piece of work and definitely wardroom material! The girl singer, her voice like the delicate trill of a lonely songbird, launched into the song 'Little Sir Echo'. D.H. was invited by the girl to make the response at the end of each line, which he attempted in fine fashion!

'Little Sir Echo, how do you do?' she trilled sweetly!

'Allo, Allo,' returned a gruff, brutal, voice, from the hulking D.H. The room burst into loud laughter and with each succeeding response, the laughter grew in volume until we literally rolled in the aisles, tears streaming uncontrollably down our faces! D.H. shuffled, he sweated, his face turned brick red as manfully he ploughed on through the interminable responses and we fell about helplessly! That slip of a girl inadvertently had exacted complete and utter revenge for all the bullying we had suffered at the hands of the tyrant and thereafter, any attempt to achieve his former domination was met by a deep, 'Allo, Allo', at which he slunk away, muttering darkly! Eventually, we settled down happily to sleep with a warm inner glow, oblivious to the hazards and happenings of the night outside the hostel at the end of what had turned out to have been a truly memorable day!

Early next morning, we rose, washed, breakfasted, packed our belongings and stumbled sleepily through the still, darkened streets, towards the docks and the ship that was to carry us on the next stage of our long journey to adventure and our eventual destination, still unknown to us. *Hectoria* was her name! A five thousand ton Norwegian factory whaling ship with a Norwegian crew who, rather than surrender to the Germans on the fall of their beloved country, had sailed through dangerous dark seas to the comparative safety of a British port, from where they continued the struggle against the hated, common enemy Germany! Her hull was painted black, her upperworks white and a huge 'gate' at the stern, through which the unfortunate, captured whale was hauled hydraulically by giant winches up a steep slope on to the cutting deck, where the huge carcass was reduced to manageable chunks, melted down into the valuable oils much in demand on the commercial markets in peacetime. Huge tanks were between decks, above which a gangway ran fore and aft, providing access to our mess-deck, forr'd and the 'dining hall' aft. Although the tanks were now empty, the ship ploughed her lonely furrow between Britain and the USA, carrying vital supplies for the war effort; when rough seas pounded the vessel during our journey, the oily odour which arose as we passed along the gangway could have deterred any but ever-hungry boys, from completing the journey at mealtimes. We stowed our kit in the foc'sle messdeck, formally the crew's quarters, each diving for the particular bunk that suited us, top, middle or bottom and without ado proceeded to explore the ship, eagerly examining every nook and cranny, including the dining-hall (very important) washing facilities and other necessities of life on board. We turned in at about ten o'clock that night, weary from the excitement of the day, only to be awakened by the throb, throb, of ships engines and the creaking, rolling motion as she powerfully met the challenge of yet another ocean voyage!

We steamed steadily to the North, avoiding the routes traversed by so many convoys, a ship alone on the endless wastes of the sea. Day after day we ploughed ever onwards, life on board settling into a steady pattern. Turn out, wash, breakfast, perhaps a spell at lookout duty, (voluntary) lunch, card playing, or reading in the mess, or any of the myriad means of passing time when at sea to alleviate the sheer boredom.

# CHAPTER THREE

*Childhood.*

I was born in the maternity wing of the Queen Mary Hospital, Plaistow, in the East End of London, on 29th of December 1924. Arriving four days late, I had the good sense not to 'turn up' on time and thus avoided the awful sentence of being called 'Noel' for the rest of my days! Had I but known what lay ahead in the 'early years' I would probably have stayed where I was, snug and comfortable, but life has to move on, so I entered this 'cruel' world screaming and howling in protest!

I was the second son, by some fourteen months, in what was eventually a family of six children, nicely balanced, with three boys and three girls. We slept in one bed, boys at the top, girls at the bottom, which had the great advantage in that sometimes we were very hot, but, at least, were never very cold.

We two boys, at that stage, had the doubtful 'distinction' of having been expelled from two schools in spite of being strictly brought up. On the first occasion, in the infants, I was forced to play in the school 'orchestra', and being tone deaf and quite shy, was relegated to playing the triangle. At the end of what must have been an excruciating performance and the usual dutiful, parental clapping, prizes were presented to some members of the orchestra, which, unfortunately, didn't include me. I thereupon bit the teacher with some force and pandemonium ensued. We were quickly removed from the school and our parents told 'Don't bring them back. Ever!'

We started at the second school somewhat under a cloud, I believe! What happened there was really Dad's fault! He taught us from an early age to look after each other and that an attack on one brother was an attack on both! A bigger boy struck one of us (after so long I don't remember which) so we both waited for him after school and when he appeared, set about him with some force, then tore off his coat, filled it with horse dung, which lay conveniently near and having tied the coat sleeves together, sent him on his way, definitely not rejoicing! That evening, seeking to be as inconspicuous as possible, we were suddenly aware of a thunderous knocking at the front door. Dad was shaving (he used a 'cut-throat' razor) but he came through from the kitchen and opened the door. There, in a blaze of fury, stood the father of the boy whom we had 'chastised'. Dad, still clutching his faithful cut-throat, his face half covered with lather, must have looked an impressive sight. Angry words were exchanged, but unfortunately, no blows and the furious father marched off! Here it comes we thought, retribution was at hand, but surprisingly, when we hurriedly explained the attack on our 'person', Dad was mollified and saying sternly, 'I told you to take care of each other', returned to the kitchen and his interrupted shave. Next day, we were taken to the headmaster's office, our parents sent for and we were off to yet another school where we must have settled down peacefully because no more such tales were ever heard of.

I remember some years later, in the summer, we two older boys were packed off to the local park, threatened with dire consequences if we didn't look after the girls, who accompanied us, properly and told to make a day of it. This was quite strange, but we set off happily enough. The youngest son, Eric, who was about eighteen months old, hadn't been seen by us for a couple of days, but no-one had told us anything about his well-being or otherwise. We returned from the park tired and dirty and on walking up the back path, looked through the window into the 'parlour', where, to our astonishment, groups of people, all dressed in black, were sitting around, with solemn faces, eating and drinking. Someone saw our dirty, puzzled faces, peering into the room and rushed out to escort us upstairs out of the way. We were told, much later, that brother Eric had died suddenly and what we had seen that sad day had been the funeral 'reception'.

We moved house to Forest Gate close by and lived in a flat above what was then called an 'oil shop', which basically sold paraffin, but also firewood, cleaning utensils and a general hotchpotch of items for the home. In the adjoining flat, lived 'Uncle Bob, Aunt Dolly' and their three children, to whom, I found many years later, we were not related in any way and they were just friends of the family.

One night, fire broke out in the shop below and quickly spread to the adjoining shops. The alarm was raised and we were taken from our bed, down the back stairs, to safety. Dad looked around and saw Bob and Dolly, but no kids. Apparently, the parents had made good their escape, leaving the children behind. Dad rushed back into the blazing building, by now well alight, fought his way upstairs and rescued the children. Newspaper reporters were soon on the scene and Dad was the hero of the hour. With typical 'Garrod' modesty he never mentioned the incident, afterwards, but, much later, when going through his old Navy 'ditty box', I came across an old, faded copy of the 'Daily Mirror' with his handsome features displayed on the front page with the caption, 'Hero rescues children from shop inferno'.

We were now homeless, with all our furniture and family possessions destroyed, but the local council came swiftly to the rescue and next day, we were re-housed in a new house in Goodmayes, Essex, on a large council estate, newly built, to accommodate families moved from a slum clearance scheme in central London. Goodmayes Lane, ran roughly from Ilford to Barking and on one side of the lane stood the 'posh houses' and on the other, the sprawling council estate. Opposite the end of Mayesbrook Road, where we lived, was Browns Farm, truly a wonderland for we London 'urchins'. There, horses, cows, chickens and other wonderful farmyard creatures roamed freely and there we learned, for the first time, that a horse and cart were not a 'unit', but the horse had a life of its own away from the cart.

The house was comfortably furnished. We had a separate bedroom for the girls and we settled in quickly at the local school, Stephens Road and life, finally, became a smooth routine of pre-war, working-class life. Ernest and I joined the five Blundell boys opposite in a 'gang' and together we roamed the farmland and the woods that were part of it to our hearts content. We were never bored or 'fed up', we just never had the time and the days were far too short. There was a cigarette machine outside the 'paper shop' around the corner in Goodmayes Lane, from which, for the princely sum of one penny, three cigarettes and several red-topped matches, which could be struck on any fairly rough surface, could be extracted. So one of the gang would enter the shop and distract the shopkeeper, whilst another would work the machine and the remainder kept watch for parents or other 'difficult people'. Across the road from the shop, a deep ditch ran the length of the lane and this was our favourite spot for a crafty smoking session. Unfortunately, the farmer had a son, a fat, ugly boy who took no part in our activities, but ran, wobbling to tell his father if he saw us in the ditch smoking. One boy had an air gun and in the manner of small boys everywhere, we mounted a sentry when smoking. The gun was loaded and it was my turn on 'duty' when I observed 'fatty' approaching. He came closer and closer and, on seeing clouds of cigarette smoke rising from the ditch, shouted, 'I'll tell my Dad' and waddled off as fast as his fat, little legs would carry him. Mindful of my duty, I raised the gun and planted a pellet in his fat, joggling backside. I never dreamt that a human being could scream so loudly! and that a stumpy-legged fat boy could run so fast. I'd heard of the 'Magic Bullet', but an air-gun pellet? Ridiculous! We evacuated the ditch swiftly and vanished as if by magic, indoors, but, surprisingly, no more was heard of this incident.

About this time, I fell in love (the first of many times) with a beautiful girl called Marie Evans, who lived further down Mayesbrook Road, on the other side. She was about nine years old, with green sparkling eyes and long, black hair. I worshipped her and followed her everywhere. Then, I made a 'fatal' mistake, carried away by the power of love. There was no swearing in our house and I never heard my father swear in all of his life, but, at school I overheard a bigger boy, when discussing a girl, say to his mate, 'I'd like to fuck her'. 'The operative word must have made a great impression on naive, little me, for I decided to send my beloved a note to declare my undying love. In my sublime innocence, I wrote, 'Dear Marie, I would like to fuck you,' then slipped it through her letter box, feeling very proud of myself! Not for long! Her mother arrived, eyes blazing, at our front door and all hell broke loose. To her mother I was a foul, depraved brute seeking to seduce her innocent little girl and should be locked up, securely for a very long time! Mum and Dad were amazed that their quiet, well brought-up son, could be such an animal! Dad, an ex-matelot and wise in the ways of a corrupt world, spoke quietly and enquired where I had heard such foul language and when I told him the origin of the offending phrase, he was very understanding and said that if any other strange words cropped up, I was to tell him and he would explain them to me! So my first venture into the realms of love ended in abject failure and was sufficient of a shock to put me off girls, for at least a couple of days, but I resolved to do better next time! Mum and Dad decided that it would be easier to keep me out of mischief if my leisure hours were filled with useful activities and as a blind piano tuner, in nearby Goodmayes Lane, was seeking a youngster to guide him around after school and all day Saturday, they took me around to meet him. We took to each other right away and so the job was mine!

Thereafter, straight home from school, no dallying with girls, have tea and round the corner to Mr Burleigh, then off to work! We walked around Becontree and Dagenham during the weekdays and travelled further afield at weekends by bus, me guiding and him tuning pianos in many places, mostly schools, halls and in private homes. I enjoyed that time so much and Mr. Burleigh proved to be a gentle, kindly man, who really appreciated my help. People that we visited were so kind and were impressed that such a young boy should be the 'seeing eye', enabling a blind man to travel where he willed, lead a full life and be gainfully employed.

Every morning, at breakfast, Mrs. Burleigh, who was herself only partially sighted, would read her husband the daily newspapers, picking out points of interest, be it politics, sport, or general gossip and he was, subsequently, very well informed, so much so that sometimes when he left the room, perhaps to use the toilet, a customer would whisper to me, 'Is he really blind?', after carrying on a deep and comprehensive conversation with him. I assured them that he was totally blind after several accidents, such as falling out of a tree when he was a young lad.

His courage and tenacity in overcoming his disability impressed me tremendously and I can never forget those instructive and happy times spent in his company, travelling around London, through Blackwall Tunnel in an open backed bus around Greenwich, Woolwich and even to an actor's flat in Maida Vale and seeing the 'great man' dressed in a long silk, dressing gown, although it was daytime and smoking a cigarette through an ornate holder with impressive elegance!

Time passed and Ernest was off to the Royal Hospital School and soon it would be my turn. Mr. Burleigh pleaded with my father to keep me at home, offering, when I was old enough, to have me taught to drive a car and even be part of the business, but to no avail. Dad's mind was made up and, eventually, off to Holbrook I went and I never saw Mr. Burleigh again!

My paternal grandfather was born with one leg shorter than the other and as not much could be done to correct that deformity in those days, he had to wear a surgical boot to 'even things up'. This in no way impaired his performance sexually for he sired fourteen offspring (that we know of) and according to surviving members of his family, he disappeared to Twickenham at most weekends, though no one seemed to know for what purpose. He died at the early age of forty-eight and on the death certificate, which I have seen, cause of death was recorded as tuberculosis, but, in my humble opinion, he was 'plumb wore out'! My father, Ernest, was the oldest child, so together, he and Grandma, set out to raise the family, which, to their eternal credit, they accomplished with great success. There was no family allowance in those far-off days and none of the myriad support agencies that exist today, but they buckled down to work and brought them up to observe the strict moral code that existed in working-class families at that time. As they became old enough, they worked hard, supported their mother and each other to the hilt, lived a close, happy, family life and till the day they died, were never heard to utter a bad word about any other member of the family. My grandmother's origins were shrouded in mystery and I could find nothing to indicate how she and her husband first met. Her father was skipper of a clipper ship, plying between England, India and Australia, that I did find out, but how two youngsters from disparate ends of the then rigid social scale met and fell in love, no one will ever know now!

My father had very definite ideas on how boys and girls should be brought up! Girls were to be treated like delicate flowers, to be nurtured and protected at all times and shielded from the harsh realities of life. Boys, on the other hand, had to be hard, worldly and fully capable of defending themselves and their interests at all times. In support of this theory, he purchased two pairs of boxing gloves and proceeded to teach us the 'noble art'. Each Sunday evening, the table was cleared from the centre of the room and with Dad as referee, we 'got stuck in'. Trouble was, however, that brother Ernest, was fourteen months older than I and much bigger and stronger! Consequently, Sunday night meant 'thumping' night for yours truly and very soon, instead of looking forward to a Sunday 'rest' day, after my 'seeing eye' labours of the week, I came to dread that day above all others and found, in latter years, that it was difficult to drop off to sleep on Sunday night without the feel of leather belting my battered nose! When Ernest went off to Holbrook, I wouldn't say that I was glad to see him go, but Sunday nights definitely became much more enjoyable for young Sam! Looking back, I can see that Dad was dead right and without that early 'training', life would have been even more 'difficult' than it proved to be! Boxing, as with football, opened many doors for me and after many fights, both in and out of the ring and my only 'souvenir', a faint scar over the left eye, although some might say, 'brain damage' too. I don't now regret that violence on a 'Holy day' which caused me so much pain many years ago! Boxing, too, creates a sense of self confidence and self reliance in a young boy and very rarely do you find that a man trained in the noble art, takes advantage of that training outside the ring to bully, or oppress others not so fortunate!

In October 1937, an official looking envelope dropped through the letter box in Mayesbrook Road. All day Mum looked at it, turned it over, put it down, then picked it up and looked again, but she didn't open it! She waited until Dad came home from work and let him open it. The letter was from the Superintendent of the Royal Hospital School, accepting Dad's application, on my behalf, to join the school. Mum promptly burst into tears; she was to lose another son, the one closest to her heart. We always had a close affinity, although she loved her 'brood' intensely and I believe would have died for any one of them, should it prove necessary! Entrance was subject to passing a written and a physical examination, which was to take place at Greenwich on November 3$^{rd}$, 1937. Mum had convinced herself that I would not pass the medical, probably because she did not want me to go!

Days passed and the fateful time to leave arrived. After a tearful farewell from Mum, Dad and I caught the bus to Greenwich and arriving in good time, reported in the designated building near the Naval College. The medical came first, then back to the waiting area where Dad sat patiently! Then, after a short interval, we boys trooped, somewhat apprehensively, into the examination room, sat down at a desk and the exam began. I don't remember anything particularly difficult about it, for Dad, despite his early struggles helping Grandma to raise the family, had always been an avid reader and was a very well, self-educated man, with a deep love and knowledge of classical music, had always encouraged us to read 'good' books and to take an interest in what went on in the world about us.

The exam was over! We were told to proceed to lunch, return at the stated time, when all would be revealed to us. Off we went, Dad and I, into Greenwich for a quick lunch. I was too excited to eat much, so Dad purchased two cheese cakes, my current favourite 'goody' and I ate both of them, helped down by a cup of hot, sweet tea. It was soon time to return, so back we traipsed to the office building, where we waited impatiently for the result of the morning exams.

'The names I shall call, are the successful candidates', a uniformed official announced, importantly, 'and should proceed to the bus outside, for the journey to Holbrook'. This was it! No hanging about, straight into the bus and off! He went down the list alphabetically and we both tensed as 'the voice' went on! Then my name was called! My heart jumped! Dad wrapped me in a bear-hug and looked shaken. Perhaps he, too, shared Mum's belief that I wouldn't make it! Then, with another quick hug and a wry smile, I was gone! Off to a new life, which was to lead me on a long trail of travel, excitement, danger and sex, not a bad prospect for a 'simple' lad, from the back streets of the 'Smoke'! Holbrook was to be my home for the next three years and Dad's strict training stood me in good stead during those years.

We were assigned to 'Nelson' house, where all new entrants (nozzers) were kitted out, taught the basics of school life and generally prepared for the eventual move to a house which would be a permanent home during our time at the school. Time passed and I was transferred to 'Collingwood House', which, like the others, housed eighty boys, between the ages of twelve to fifteen, in two dormitories of forty boys, each supervised firstly by Petty-officer boys, with a Chief Petty-officer boy in overall charge, responsible in turn to the housemaster, who had a flat in the building.

Our domestic and medical needs were provided by a matron and this was where I fell in love, deeply and passionately, for the second time! First sight of Sister Ross, in her crisp, neat uniform and heard her gentle voice, like the tinkling of a thousand silver bells and my youthful heart was hers, forever!

She taught us to 'make and mend'; to sew, darn socks, to iron clothes, to behave like gentlemen, though, I must confess, from the safety of the long years between, at times I had anything but a gentleman's fantasy about her graceful, lovely person! When the time came for me to leave the school, I just could not face saying 'goodbye' to her, for I was afraid it would all end in tears: mine!

The history of the Royal Hospital School has been comprehensively chronicled in three, excellent books by H.D. Turner in 1980; by Philip Newell in 1984 and again, by H.D. Turner in 1990, so I will not delve into that history except to record the establishment of the School in 1694 by William III and his wife, Queen Mary, following the great naval victory over the French, at the Battle of La

Hogue in 1692, as a provision for the 'maintenance and education of the children of seamen, happening to be slain, or disabled, in such service'. It is administered by the Board of Admiralty and has been known for many years as the 'Cradle of the Navy'.

The Superintendent, in 1937, was Captain Evan Bruce-Gardyne, Royal Navy, who looked a formidable figure to the boys, but I personally found him to be quite a kindly gentleman beneath that rugged exterior, who genuinely had the interests of the boys at heart.

The chaplains were the very best that I encountered anywhere and were to me, rather like 'big brothers', keen sportsmen, and totally unlike the wimps that most matelots wouldn't go to for advice or assistance, however dire their problems

The seamanship and gunnery instructors were strict but fair and, looking back, I thought that they, too, were the best of their breed and had obviously been chosen for boys service with great care! Collingwood housemaster, whose name I sadly cannot remember, was approachable, very helpful and carried out his duties with quiet efficiency. I even sparred with him several times before fights and he gave as good as he got, but without taking advantage of his superior height and weight. I both liked and respected him, unlike many of those in authority I encountered later in my career! We were lavishly kitted out with just about everything an active youngster could require, both domestically and on the sports field.

I revelled in the sports facilities, 'scoffed' the food, while others complained, and luxuriated in my own bed, hard though it undoubtedly was. I wasn't too keen on climbing the 100ft. mast, but after a while, became used to it, although it was 'bloody awful' in winter, or in the cold winds that swept the school across the vast open space of the playing fields. Sometimes, a boy would upset the P.T.I. whilst doing P.T. and he would scream, 'Way you go, up the mast, up the east side, down the west side', and off you would go, clad only in thin P.T. gear. Out the gym door, across the parade ground and, teeth chattering, up the mast. On occasion, I would grip the ratlines so hard that it was some time before my fingers thawed out and returned to normal. Some instructors favoured a 'stonecky' with which they belaboured the backside of some 'unfortunate' who couldn't run as fast as the rest, but I took good care to ensure that my 'arse' wasn't in the 'firing line'.

Old Bill in charge of the swimming pool was one of the boys' favourite characters and I remember him with affection. He had been severely wounded in the Dardennelles campaign during World War I, but used to ride his old pushbike to work every day. He organised the early boys in the baths, to open the end door which led directly into the building at the deep end every morning, which they did and he rode majestically in, wheeled right along the edge of the pool to his office. One morning, however, things went disastrously wrong for poor old Bill.

His faithful 'bike' skidded on the wet poolside, and Bill and the bike plunged into the cool water and vanished with a last flurry beneath the surface. Some lads dived in immediately in a gallant rescue attempt, when, suddenly, Bill's balding head broke the surface. He was in magnificent form! Swear words spilled from his shivering lips in an unending stream. The air turned blue, paintwork blistered, even the water in the pool heated up (for the first and only time in the three years that I spent at Holbrook).

My class arrived at this time and an incredible sight greeted our amazed eyes! There stood this respected figure, gaunt and scarred, with only a towel clutched about his slender waist, directing the 'rescue' of his beloved friend' from the murky depths of the deep end. This incident passed into school folklore and, fortunately, Old Bill, seemed none the worse for his unexpected 'ducking'. I remember one other 'incident' which took place in the baths. It was customary every year to have a Sports Day when the school was open to visitors. High at one end of the pool was a spectators gallery, which, on this occasion, was filled with visiting parents, curious locals and school officials with their wives, girlfriends and children. On 'normal' days we were not allowed to wear any item of clothing whilst using the pool, but on open days, competitors wore a small 'slip', which barely covered the 'wedding tackle'. One of our 'bigger' boys, McCarthy, who later held several swimming titles, easily won his freestyle race. On reaching the pools end, he swung gracefully from the water, to meet the cheers of his admiring fans. Hands above his head, he acknowledged the storm of cheering which was even louder than usual! The cheers and laughter reached a deafening crescendo and puzzled, he glanced downward! There was his 'generous' manhood, swinging gently in the warm air and suddenly, he had many more admiring fans and his only cover, embarrassment! I worked hard in the classroom, on the parade and the sports field, but I did well, basically, because I enjoyed it and hated to be surpassed by anyone at anything! Soon, I was noticed by the powers that be and uprated to Petty Officer Boy, second in charge of forty boys, and with quite a responsibility toward them. We marched the 'lads' to the dining hall for breakfast, dinner and supper and outside that building, one day, came the first challenge to my authority. My boys were the youngest and so the smallest group in the house and the older, bigger boys lived in similar accommodation, on the other side of the building. Their PO Boy at that time was a red-headed Scots firebrand, called Vic, who obviously fancied his chances with me, as I was his junior in length of service as PO Boy. We had halted outside the dining hall awaiting our turn to enter. Standing quietly at ease, my lads were suddenly ploughed into by Vic's group of bigger boys. This was very unusual as, generally, we had a mutual respect for one another, in order to uphold our position of responsibility and I felt like smashing my fist into his grinning face! Fortunately and uncharacteristically, I did not, but using the tradition of the school, chose to challenge him to a fight in the lower shower room, the accepted venue for all disputes that could only be settled by fisticuffs and, there after supper, we met in 'mortal combat'. Honour was at stake, both mine and that of the junior 'side', so I was determined to show him no mercy. The shower room was packed with boys of all sizes, some were unable to get inside, so their anxious faces peered through the windows.

We were evenly matched in size, etc., but I quickly got to work with a flurry of heavy blows. After a few minutes of this pressure and looking already somewhat battered, he'd had enough and in the tradition of such fights, said so! Honour and Sam Garrod were satisfied!

The 'fight' with Vic did me a power of good. Instead of 'slagging off' one another, we had settled the dispute quickly and decisively in time-honoured fashion. Word quickly spread, I was the hero of the 'youngsters' and no other 'challengers' appeared! Members of staff mentioned the incident obliquely and seemed quite pleased with the outcome.

Smoking was a most heinous offence in the school and although I personally never 'indulged', many boys did so. The penalty for being caught was, in my opinion, nothing short of barbaric for that day and age. First offence, six cuts of the cane, second offence, twelve cuts, carried out in the best traditions of Captain Bligh!

The unfortunate culprit was escorted to the gym, stripped to just a pair of thin P.T. shorts and then hauled over a vaulting buck, with wrists and ankles held firmly, by two burly P.T.I.s. The Commander was present with the Medical Officer, and a brawny instructor wielded the cane. The instructor would turn to the Commander, salute and say, 'Request to carry out punishment, Sir?'

Commander to Medical Officer: 'Is this boy fit to receive punishment, Doctor?'

Medical Officer to Commander: 'Fit, Sir,' he dutifully replied!

Commander to Instructor: 'Carry on punishment.'

'Aye, Aye, Sir,' replied the instructor, turning toward the, by now, terrified boy and, cane in hand, flexed his bulging muscles. Down came the cane with a swish as it cut through the air, striking the boy's buttocks with the weight of a sixteen stone man behind it! 'One, Sir, Two Sir,' intoned the instructor with each successive blow, until all cuts 'awarded', had been struck!

'Punishment completed,' said the instructor with a salute.

'Carry on, please,' replied the Commander and off he went for a quiet drink and a pleasant evening with the family, his 'duty' done! The suffering boy was escorted to the Sick Bay, examined, then returned to his house.

This is one example of the way in which young boys (the oldest would be just fifteen years of age) were treated by their seniors, certainly not their superiors. Any reader who wishes to doubt the truth of what I have written, please contact my brother, who, at age seventy-one, probably still carries the scars of his barbaric caning, psychologically, if not physically, so many years ago! His offence? Carving his initials in the mess room table. Stupid, but hardly meriting such sadistic treatment in a supposedly civilised country!

The scenario depicted above, had hardly changed from that in the days of the 'Bounty' and the notorious Captain Bligh, although of course, not being lashed to a grating and beaten with a cat o'nine tails, could be considered significant progress in some quarters!

I continued to work hard, do well in sport, progress favourably in the classroom and, in reward, was promoted to Chief Petty Officer Boy, in charge of the whole house of eighty boys! The pinnacle of achievement at Holbrook and the happiest moment of my life, so far!

All boys, in those days, at Holbrook wore flannel night-shirts to bed, which came down to just under the knees. C.P.O. boys had the 'special' privilege of a long night-shirt. On first joining, these night-shirts took some getting used to and itched like the very devil, but after a while, we found them to be both warm and comfortable. Another privilege was being invited to the housemaster's flat in the evening after the boys were in bed. Alternate weekends, the invitation was to spend a few hours with matron, to which I looked forward impatiently! The evening took the form of a chat about the house, in general and some boys, in particular, especially boys who had difficulty settling in, were homesick, or were not good mixers. Sandwiches, tea and cakes were provided and much appreciated by yours truly.

One other privilege accorded C.P.O. Boys was that of taking local leave on Sunday, between the hours of completion of the midday meal and 1800 hours. All other boys left the confines of the school only for seasonal leave, or organised outings, for sport or educational purposes, so local leave was a rare privilege, indeed and much appreciated by the recipients. On the first Sunday, I arranged with my 'oppo', 'Rabbo' Humphries, a stroll through the woods down by the village, so after lunch, making sure the 'mess' was cleaned up and 'squared away', we set off with springing step and light hearts, through the school and down the road to the woods. In my wildest dreams, I never imagined that on returning, my heart would be singing, but my step would have much less spring in it! Taking the narrow path, through the woods, we came upon two young girls, sitting on the trunk of a fallen tree. They were about sixteen years old I reckoned, and one was quite pretty, with blonde hair, blue eyes and a shapely bust, on which my hungry eyes fastened as if by magic. To my astonishment, she opened her comely lips and said, in a low voice, 'I know you, you're Sam Garrod, the boxer!' Alarm bells rang in my head! Some bastards been using my name! 'Not guilty', I answered quickly, 'you've got the wrong person'. 'What's the matter?' she said curiously. 'My Dad took me and my brother to see you fight in the gym.' I immediately relaxed and she then said, 'I enjoyed it and you are very athletic'. The other girl giggled and I thought: 'that one's yours, Rabbo!'

With typical Garrod modesty, I said, 'I'm athletic, but you're beautiful', at which she had the grace to blush demurely! 'Shall we go for a walk', said she, with a meaningful glance at her friend, who immediately grabbed hold of Rabbo's arm and led him off in the opposite direction, which saved us the difficulty of making a choice and suited me admirably!

'My name is Claire and I already know yours', she said, as we walked through a gap in the bushes and into a small, grassy glade. I'll have to be careful here, I thought, but as it happened, there was nothing to fear. We sat on the grass and her slim, soft fingers stroked my bare leg (we wore shorts, until we left Holbrook) moving higher and higher, as we talked. I was as hard as a 'Japanese rock cake' and I gently, but with trembling fingers, undid her blouse and bared her budding breasts. I thought, ol' Rabbo will never believe this, but what did I know? I always believed in helping people, so I lifted up my bum from the cool soft, grass and quickly slid my shorts down around the ankles. She sighed deeply and gently kissed the throbbing head. 'I shall always call you 'Nobby',' she whispered softly (I was circumcised when a young baby) and that name has stuck with him ever since! She gently, but firmly, stroked ol' Nobby, who thought it was Christmas and birthday, all in one go. Her hand moved faster and faster and, finally, it was more than flesh and blood could stand and Nobby let go! Such was the force of the emission that I swear it brought down a fly meandering innocently by. It never had a chance! Before I had recovered, Claire said, huskily, 'See you next Sunday' and buttoning her blouse, rose gracefully to her feet. 'You bet', I croaked, frightened to move with an empty spine! 'You're lovely', she said, with some feeling and who was I to disagree! That night, I fell asleep in the chapel for the first time ever, during evensong and the duty master, who knew me well, said in a concerned voice, 'You're looking tired, Garrod, try not to do so much'. But what did he know?

Claire and I met regularly that idyllic summer. We explored the soft, intimate curves of our firm, young bodies, made love, innocently and with great passion, under clear, blue skies in our hidden woodland glade.

This was the happiest time of my life and the 'black dog' of loneliness, which had dogged me since leaving home, receded into the background, before the sheer power of this all-embracing love! After leaving Holbrook, Claire and I were never to meet again, but years afterward, during the long, cold watches of the night, memories of the time we spent together came flooding back and a warm glow spread throughout my tired, chilled body. Wherever you are, my love, I pray the 'Gods' have been kind to you over the intervening years and that you have found the sublime happiness which you so truly deserve!

Prize day at the school and we were all gathered together in Assembly to receive our reward for hard work, both in the classroom and on the sports field. I received a R.L.S.S. Certificate and medallion, accolades for football, cricket, shooting and a medal for boxing, plus a mention for achieving twelfth place in the senior cross-country race. The greatest and most prestigious prize of all, the coveted Proficiency Badge was also mine! On my final appearance on the stage, as Captain Bruce-Cardyne shook my hand, he remarked, with a smile, 'Is there anything you cannot do, Garrod?' My heart was bursting with pride and I thought, if only Mum and Dad were here now!

Thinking back on those days, several memories were imprinted on my mind! The swimming bath, where, on winter mornings, the boys stood shivering and 'Old Bill' would say, 'What's wrong with you boy?'

'The water's cold, sir.'

'Get me the thermometer, boy,' he always replied.

Off scampered the lad to the office, where the 'infamous' instrument was stored. On his return, Bill, would gently lower it into the water, on its length of bleached line, haul it out again and say, in a mock, stern voice. 'You, boy, read it', and this the boy did, although all present knew it would register at seventy-two degrees, as it never failed to do in my three years at Holbrook.

Each and every morning, snuggled in a warm bed, there would sound off a loud 'clang', as the large key, which turned on the water supply to the showers, went home, and at that sound, forty boys would leap from bed, tear off their flannel night-shirt and run naked to the showers, which were always cold. A vigorous rub down, on completion, back to the dorm, hurriedly dress, make your own bed, line up the bed-chocks, downstairs and ready for the first of the days marches to the dining-hall. That was the routine, day in, day out, as I remember it!

Sunday, on the parade ground, marching to the tunes of the boys' own band, shouted commands and instructions. Inspection, sometimes by a visiting dignitary, who usually addressed the parade with a few words of praise for a smart turn-out, then march off to church, for morning service.

At last, time to leave Holbrook, with its happy memories and a place that had become my home, whilst my 'real' home was now just where I went for leave periods and pedalled my 'trade bike' delivering meat for the local butcher 'to pass away the time'. I used to assist the butcher's young, attractive wife make the sausages in the back room and, many times, when her plump, pink-fingers, swiftly and expertly, 'worked' the 'skin' on to the nozzle of the sausage making machine, 'ol Nobby' grew restless and obviously longed to be back in Holbrook's 'leafy glade'.

# CHAPTER FOUR

*Hectoria at sea.*

Hectoria ploughed purposefully on, her powerful engines and sturdy hull easily rebuffing the advances of restless seas that strove to deviate her from her chosen course, but there was a different note to those engines now, as if the ship herself knew that the end of her long journey was in sight, and that, shortly, she would be resting safely alongside a harbour wall.

Her crew moved about the ship with a cheerful, springy step, previously lacking, their seaman's mind, obviously buoyed up by the promised delights and there were many of yet another bustling seaport.

We were, as usual, told nothing, but the dhobying was brought up to date, unnecessary items stowed away and we prepared for our long-awaited next move, on the next stage of the journey, which proved to be shoreside, in Halifax, Nova Scotia.

We prepared to disembark, excitedly, but then the blow fell! The ship taking our party to Bermuda (the next stage) had berths for only eighteen boys. Two boys had to travel by alternate transport and, cruelly, for us, it was decided that Tom and I were those two boys. It was a bitter blow, but, fortunately, at the time, we had no idea what difference that decision would make to our lives, in the short term.

Off the lads went, happy in the knowledge that they, at least, were still together. Tom and I, with heavy hearts and a strange sense of foreboding, were transported to a nearby Armed Merchant Cruiser, *HMS California*, which was to be our home for a few days, until the elderly battleship, *HMS Revenge*, arrived in harbour. We stowed our kit, wandered about the ship and no one bothered us with duties or routine. *California*, was clean, comfortable and the food was good, but shortly, all was to change!

*Revenge* lumbered into harbour, secured alongside and we 'humped' the inevitable kitbag and hammock on board. What a difference, in every respect! Back to the shouted orders and harsh treatment that we had hoped was far behind us. We were bullied, treated like morons and generally browbeaten; and that was only the officers! That first night, on board, an invitation had been extended to the Ship's company to what was known as a 'cake and arse' party, which meant there was no booze, no 'crumpet' available and generally, a pretty boring evening for most matelots. There were no volunteers, so rather than upset the sponsors with a refusal of hospitality, Tom and I were detailed off to attend! Clad in our, by now, crumpled No 1s (they had been in our kitbags for weeks) we were transported to the party venue. We stood there like two 'lemons' amid this group of 'posh' people, who, to be fair to them, were determined to give us a good time. Talk about uncomfortable! Two working-class youngsters pitched unwillingly into a lifestyle we had seen only in the cinema and hating every minute of it. As I stood shyly there, trying to hide behind Tom (he was doing the same, behind me) our enormous hostess seized hold of me by the 'lower band' and practically lifted my reluctant frame on to the dance floor. Now, I couldn't dance a step, but she clutched me to her overhanging bosom (I couldn't even see where we were going) and dragged me around the floor.

I struggled to breathe, but as the delicate aroma of her expensive perfume exuded from between her mighty breasts, I am deeply ashamed to record that 'Ole Nobby' started to take an interest and rise to the occasion! What a player! He certainly was getting hungry and only great embarrassment in sight! Fortunately, my hostess decided at this point that enough was enough and guiding us back to the 'picking up' point, let me go! Strangely enough, she appeared to have enjoyed her perambulations around the floor, whether that was due to 'Nobby's' rigid presence, I know not, but she positively beamed at me and that certainly wasn't down to my dancing ability! Tom's only comment on my performance was to say, 'How did you get that white powder on your nose?' I just grinned, weakly, in reply! Eventually, we staggered exhausted and miserable back on board, slung our hammocks on the sponson deck and drifted, unhappily, off to sleep!

Next day was even worse than that previous, but, at least, the ship was under way, which was a more hopeful sign that our ordeal might soon be over. I was detailed off as gangway messenger, which normally would have been not too bad, but once the watertight doors and hatches were closed, I was lost! It was like being blindfolded in a maze and trying to get out. Any decent person would have sent someone to find me but no! there I was, wandering about, with a message to deliver, somewhere and no idea where I was. Finally the working period came to an end and I managed to find my way back to the mess.

Poor Tom had had an even worse time, scrubbing out the messdeck, driven by some heartless bastard, who delighted in making his life a misery. He sat down in the evening and wrote a desperate appeal to his father, in far-off Gravesend, to buy him out immediately, if not, he threatened to commit suicide! That bit really scared me! Tom was no 'mamby pamby' boy from 'civvy street', but one who had been raised the hard way, both at home and on T.S. Arethusa and was used to life's hard times. Next morning at reveille, I quickly raised myself in my hammock and looked to make sure he was still there and not hanging from some hammock rail. Strangely, his utter misery helped me to overcome my own and there and then I decided that those bastards were not going to beat me! Thereafter, I 'walked' around the ship and took my time. When some 'pig' of an officer shouted, I didn't let it bother me and thought what I would like to do to him, if we were on equal terms!

On the messdeck, with its cluster of lagged pipes and myriad dark corners, the cockroaches reigned supreme! They were everywhere and there was no escape from their disgusting presence. Some boys, used to roll up sheets of newspaper, set fire to them and jam the flaming paper behind the fanshafts or pipes. There issued forth a horrible, crackling sound and the burning cockroaches scuttled everywhere. My flesh crawled at the sight and sound.

At last, the journey came to an end and *Revenge* came to anchor off Hamilton, Bermuda. A boat came alongside to take us ashore and never, in all my naval career, have I been so glad to leave a ship! It was hell! It severely dented our ambitions for the future and I decided that if that was the Navy, 'they' could keep it!

The constant psychological abuse of boys in the Royal Navy was a national disgrace and when one considers that these youngsters serving at sea in time of war were officially 'not there', for their 'engagement' toward pension and promotion rights didn't commence until after their eighteenth birthday! Shells, bombs, torpedoes and even Germans were not 'selective' where age was concerned and possibly hundreds of boys were lost at sea, as were some of my class, when according to their 'Lordships', sitting comfortably in their cosy offices in London they weren't 'officially' there at all! Great changes have indeed taken place in conditions of 'Boys service', but nothing has been done to redress the injustices dealt to those youngsters, who died, or served their country, in its greatest hour of need!

We set foot on the beautiful Island of Bermuda, at last. The air was warm and balmy, the sun shone brightly and our dimmed spirits began to lift. Tom and I had arrived before the main body of boys and quite frankly, everyone we met seemed amazed that lads so young should be here at all in such dangerous times. We were billeted in the Fleet Air Arm pilots' mess, and they treated us with kindness and consideration. We had no duties as such, but we helped in the mess and one day, volunteered to assist the 'bin man', who drove one of the few lorries on the island, collected the bins on the base and took them for disposal on the dump. Soon, the main party arrived and settled in with us!

What a tale they had to tell! Their vessel, in direct contrast to ours, was a Canadian, luxury cruise liner, plying between Halifax, New York and Bermuda, with a passenger list of rich Canadians and Americans vacationing in Bermuda, and once they knew the boys' story and that they were serving in the Royal Navy, their generosity knew no bounds! The lucky lads were showered with gifts of ice cream, cartons of cigarettes and even wined and dined with their benevolent hosts until the whole voyage seemed more like a dream, from which they would soon awake, than a true, joyous 'happening'. When we told of our experiences everyone wondered, deep down, if our final move to the battleship, *Rodney*, would be as disastrous. Anyway, that was in the future and we determined to enjoy ourselves while still we may.

There was a glorious beach nearby, Tobacco Bay, and there we played, swimming in the crystal clear sea, or lounging on the immaculate beach. Kindly ladies from the British community manned a tea-bar there and served us free teas, delicious sandwiches and wonderful cakes, some of which were homemade by them! What a glorious interlude for us and one that we would never forget!

One day, a strike by waterfront workers was announced, which meant that British corvettes based in Bermuda on anti-submarine patrol duties, which used coal for cooking purposes in their galleys and were about to return to harbour, would be unable to refuel, while the strike lasted. The barracks C.O. asked for volunteers to perform this vital task and as one 'boy' we answered his call for help! We were taken to the dockside, furnished with overalls and split into groups of about ten boys, under the supervision of a plump, coloured man called Absalom, whom we promptly re-christened 'Abso' and who was a foreman, normally in charge of local labour. He provided a two-wheeled cart, pulled by a small donkey wearing a hat, from which its ears protruded. 'Abso' pointedly told us not to overload the cart and decreed the number of bags we should place on it and off he went to see how the other groups were getting on. We set to with a will and shovelled the coal into rope-handled bags, for others to place on the cart. Suddenly, there was a loud whinny from the donkey as he shot into the air and dangled momentarily from the traces. Then the coal slid off the cart and the donkey fell back to earth with a crash and a loud scream! In their eagerness to do a good job, the lads had forgotten Abso's warning and put one too many bags on the cart, with disastrous results! We laughed and laughed and the tears rolled down our blackened faces, leaving white channels where they had flowed, which, when we saw it, made us laugh the more. Abso came rushing up, but when he saw us falling about, he hesitated and then joined in. What a day!

All good things come to an end and one day, *HMS Rodney* entered harbour, looking huge and threatening with her mighty sixteen-inch guns and unusual design. One of only two such ships, she had nine huge guns, mounted in three turrets forr'd, on a long, raking foc'sle, which earned her the name, the 'Ugly Duckling', but her spacious messdecks, sea-keeping qualities and happy atmosphere, soon put our earlier fears to rest. Yet again, we packed our kit and prepared to leave our idyllic surroundings for the unknown perils that lay ahead!

We said 'goodbye' to our friendly hosts of *HMS Malabar*, as the base was named and drove to the dockside, recent scene of our 'coaling exploits', but now we were quieter and more thoughtful, for whatever life was like on board, good or bad, we would be stuck with it for some time and short of Tom's desperate 'remedy' on board *Revenge*, there was no escape!

Our kit was loaded, by dockside workers, into a large provision net and hoisted by crane into the ship's launch, which lay alongside and then we trooped aboard and were off! *Rodney* loomed larger and larger, as we neared her vast bulk and I had a shaky feeling in my stomach! We secured alongside the gangway and the net with our kit was hoisted inboard. Curious faces lined the guardrails and many eyes watched our unsteady progress up the steep ladder. We stepped on to the deck, turning aft and saluting the quarterdeck, as we had been taught. A three badge leading seaman came forward and introduced himself to us: 'I am Leading Seaman Clark,' said he in a quiet, firm voice, 'and I am responsible for you and the running of the boys messdeck'. I felt better already! Definitely not the shouting, bawling type of leader so common in the Navy at that time, which we all abhorred.

'Right, now you know who I am, let's get your kit to the messdeck and get settled in,' he said, 'down that hatch and we'll take it from there.' Being eager to make a good impression, I leapt swiftly into action and seizing my kitbag, hurled it down the hatch pointed out by him and immediately there was a piercing yell, followed by a string of swear words, that made even our toughened ears curl. Apparently, a matelot going about his lawful business, had set foot on the ladder, only to be struck, amidships, by a flying kit bag and, naturally, he was not very pleased about it! LS Clark rose nobly to the occasion. 'These are seaman boys joining the ship, give 'em a break!' At this the damaged rating calmed down and I thought it safe to apologise, to which he replied, 'That's O.K., lad, sorry about the language,' and he demonstrated his remorse by helping us move our kit.

Our messdeck was right forr'd on the main deck and was separated by a bulkhead forr'd and a high row of lockers aft, thus making it quite secluded. It was clean, light and airy and we felt that life would be fairly comfortable within its confines. LS Clark showed us the toilets and bathroom exclusively for our use, where the mess utensils were stowed and where to sling our hammocks, in which we must be safely ensconced before nine o'clock rounds, that night! Reveille was at 0600 next morning, thirty minutes before the hands were called and we would have to lash up our hammocks, stow them in the netting and be ready for work at that time. On completion, hands to breakfast, dress in the rig of the day and fall in to be detailed for work about the ship.

I was detailed as Commander's Office messenger and that really was a stroke of luck, for I worked in and from there and for no-one else and the R.P.O. in charge was a bloke who guarded my interests jealously! My 'Action Station' was in 'B' turret, shell-handling room, deep in the very bowels of the ship and virtually locked in a steel tomb if the ship sank. At the time, we really didn't think too much about that possibility, for, to us, the mighty ship seemed capable of dealing with any 'difficulty' that arose. Oh, the confidence of youth!

The ship's company was daily piped to bathe over the side and in the clear crystal waters it was possible to see the myriad fish of all sizes, shapes and colours, that abounded there. During these periods, armed Royal Marine sharpshooters were on duty in case of shark attack and while, during our stay, no sharks did come near, the warning was sounded several times and many world swimming records were unofficially broken as nervous matelots raced for the safety of the gangway!

# CHAPTER FIVE

*HMS Rrodney*
*August, 1941.*

The battleships *Nelson* and *Rodney* owed their unusual design to limitations imposed upon Britain by the Washington Treaty. The United States Government invited the governments of Great Britain, Japan, France and Italy to attend a conference in Washington to discuss arms limitation and various other problems of the day. The Washington Conference, opened on 21$^{st}$ November, 1921 and it was agreed that no more large battleships would be built exceeding 35,000 tons displacement, or with guns larger than 16-inch, but, as American and Japanese existing battleships already carried 16-inch guns, Britain would be allowed to build two new ships of this size. *Nelson*, the flagship, at 720ft long, ten feet longer than *Rodney*, in order to provide accommodation aft for the Admiral, and *Rodney* were originally to carry main armament aft, but owing to the limitations of the new treaty, had to redesign the ships to conform to treaty specifications. Thus, the 'Ugly Ducklings' were 'born' and formidable ships they were, giving sterling service throughout World War 2 in many parts of the globe, escorting convoys, bombarding enemy positions, in support of the Army and many other tasks so important in the pursuance of modern warfare.

*Rodney* was launched in 1925, with a beam of 106ft, draught of 30ft and with a displacement of 38,000 tons (full load). Her armament consisted of nine sixteen inch guns, in three triple turrets forward, with a secondary armament of twelve dual-purpose six-inch guns in twin turrets, three on each side, aft.

Her anti-aircraft armament consisted of six 4.7 guns, forty-eight two-pounder pom-poms and sixty-one 20 millimetre cannon. She also carried two 24-inch submerged torpedo tubes, forr'd and had the distinction of having been the only battleship in history to have fired torpedoes at another battleship in action! There is no record of her having recorded a hit!

She carried two 'Walrus' amphibious aircrafts which were catapulted from a ramp 'atop' X-turret and on recovery were hoisted inboard by means of a small derrick mounted amidships.

Her speed was laid down as twenty-three knots, but, during my time onboard, she 'struggled' to achieve eighteen knots 'flat out'! *Rodney* was a comfortable, 'happy', clean ship and the boys 'carried' aboard were treated with strict discipline, but fairly and with consideration.

We kept watch, four on, four off, at sea and carried out our daily tasks exactly to the same routine as the ship's company. There was a large 'rec' space on the main deck with a NAAFI canteen selling cigarettes, chocolate (nutty), razor blades and all the usual paraphernalia of such canteens. There was also a 'gopher' bar which sold a delicious mixture consisting of lemonade, or 'pop', as it's now known, with a large 'dollop' of ice cream to top it up. It was the boys' favourite drink onboard, as we were too young to sample the delights of alcohol and instead of a daily 'tot' of rum, usually two-and-one for the ratings, we were given lime juice, which, in cold weather, did nothing to warm the 'cockles of the heart', as the tot did.

As the day to day running of a country depends largely on the state of its currency, aboard ship, at that time, the form of currency was the far from humble tot! With it, all doors could be opened and any 'difficulty' overcome. A ship, similar to *Rodney*, was like a small town and practically anything could be obtained onboard! 'Pussera' suits were made, dhobying done, boots or shoes, repaired, letters written to loved ones far away and even 'special' letters to sweethearts met ashore, who needed an overwhelming, convincing love letter to prove that she was, indeed, the true love of a lonely sailor! All 'paid' for with the tot and not a penny piece changing hands!

One of my duties from the Commander's Office involved delivering signals to various key officers' cabins and one day, I knocked on the cabin door of a particular officer, to be answered by a high pitched voice! 'Come in,' it trilled.

Confidently, in I went, only to be greeted by a strange sight! On a gaily coloured rug in the centre of the cabin stood a naked figure with ginger hair, busily spraying its body from a small perfume bottle! I had seen my sisters (though never naked, of course) using such a spray on their hair and I was flabbergasted at the very sight of such a bizarre apparition!

'Put it down, there, on the small table', intoned the delicate voice of 'Ginger'. I did exactly that, and dived out the door, in one swift movement, eager to escape from such an unseemly vision.

*Rodney* had arrived in Bermuda, directly after her visit to Boston, Mass. USA, where she had been undergoing a refit, after her success during the 'Sink the Bismark' operation, when her massive sixteen inch guns had pounded the 'Pride of the German Navy' into a blazing hulk, finally to be dispatched to 'Davy Jones's Locker' by torpedoes from *HMS Dorsetshire*.

Much has been written of that 'episode' by far more expert Naval historians than I, so I will not dwell upon it further, but, in my humble opinion, much of the credit accorded King George V in her role as flagship should have passed to *Rodney*, for her greater involvement in the action.

In Bermuda, most of the broadside messes sported twin British and American flags, decorating the shipside messkit stowage and we new arrivals were regaled, constantly, with stories of the generous hospitality of the American people and the huge quantities of food and drink, provided by them during the refit period.

There was also, at that time a 'Bundles for Britain' charity drive and huge quantities of excellent clothing, mostly female, were donated to *Rodney* and stowed inboard. We were provided with large collapsible cardboard boxes, which we made up and, at a given signal, proceeded to fill with articles from the massive pile of clothing. Having three sisters, my thoughts were naturally of them and I selected 'my share' quickly and expertly, only deviating once to pick up a knitted woollen 'scarf', which had a note affixed to it from the 'knitter', who proved to be an eighty-two year old American lady. Afterwards, all selection made, I read the note and it moved me greatly! It was handwritten, obviously with some difficulty and wished the wearer of the scarf God's protection during the dangers that lay ahead and a speedy return to loved ones. It contained an address and I wrote a short 'thank you' note in reply and posted it onboard, but no reply ever came!

Who knows what happened to that kindly lady, who despite her advancing years, still cared enough for her fellow creatures to spend time and precious energy in performing a labour of love to help comfort them! This was no ordinary scarf! It was roughly six feet long by four feet wide and during the long hours and many deadly days that lay ahead, closed up in the comfortless bowels of that great ship on convoy escort duties in the Atlantic and off Iceland, I wrapped my shivering body in that 'blanket' and blessed, with all my young heart, that lovely lady, wherever she might be!

Some time later, when I arrived home, I found that one of my 'selections' made in all innocence, had shocked my mother and she was heard to exclaim: 'He's at it again, doesn't he ever stop'? Simple sailorman that I was, I had 'selected' a pair of expensive, silk 'French knickers', as they were then called and to the end of her long life, my mother always believed I had stripped them from the delicate body of some poor victim of my insatiable lust!

# CHAPTER SIX

*HMS Rodney at sea.*

The ship left harbour and proceeded on convoy escort duties in the Atlantic. We steamed steadily northwards and out came the winter woollies, the ubiquitous duffle coat, one-piece overalls (our routine uniform dress, out of harbour) sea-boot stockings and boots. Wearing of lifebelts at sea was compulsory (common sense really) though some resented the 'inconvenience'. We boys carried on our normal duties around the ship during the day, but when the hands went to Action Stations, so did we, with a will, and though the ship's company moved swiftly, boys were usually the first to close up at their station. We were based mainly in Scapa Flow, or in Halfiord, Iceland, from where we escorted merchant men across those dangerous seas, the graveyard for many a fine ship and her brave crew, across the Atlantic to some point at which Canadian, or even American ships, took over and continued to the comparative safety of Halifax harbour, Nova Scotia.

We assumed responsibly at sea for the homeward bound convoy with its valuable cargo of essential war materials to enable Britain to continue the fight, which many countries around the world, considered to be a lost cause. Many American diplomats in Congress and throughout the American political scene thought too, at that time, that Britain was finished and would soon be occupied by the German Army and the Nazi monsters of Adolf Hitler.

Fortunately, President Roosevelt felt differently and knowing full well that if Britain collapsed, America would stand isolated in a hostile world, until it became its turn too to fall under Germany's domination, he quietly set about assisting Britain in a practical way, by making available to her the veritable lifeblood of a successful war effort by way of essential foodstuffs and armaments in increasing quantities, which were carried by many thousands of ships in convoy, despite the increasing attentions of Hitler's U-boats, across the Atlantic and the gales and storms, which so often beset our gallant Merchant Seamen. Convoy Escort was often a boring, humdrum task, until, suddenly, the peaceful scene would be shattered by a terrific explosion and a merchantman would vanish from sight in a cloud of black smoke and falling debris and, if she were carrying aviation fuel or munitions, would never be seen again.

Sometimes, men would be seen struggling in the water with rescue tugs racing to their assistance, but too often, they vanished beneath the cruel waves before they could be plucked to safety. Other times, when the smoke cleared, nothing could be seen of the ship or its luckless crew and we would all be greatly saddened and perhaps wonder, who's next!

Graceful destroyers would come bustling up and start the search for yet another U-boat, which, by now, would have gone deep, or taken swift evasive action. The 'crump, crump' of depth charges would echo across the scene and the hunters would patiently and carefully, in a well-rehearsed pattern, search beneath the surface for their hated, elusive enemy!

In the beginning, many U-boats did escape retribution, but as better trained escorts, in greater numbers, became available, the tide began to turn and the days of easy pickings were over and the lives of submarine crews became, in their turn, intolerable!

We spent months at sea, being re-fuelled under way and, having delivered one convoy, or in some cases, its remnants, were off again, this time escorting a convoy of troopships at the start of its long journey round the Cape to the Middle East.

Destination Freetown, Sierra Leone, West Africa, known in those days because of the pestilent mosquitoes as the 'white man's grave'. Malaria, prickly heat, ringworm and many of her debilitating diseases were rampant there and the heat was so intense that it seemed impossible to gain any respite from its energy-sapping breath.

As we steamed further south, the routine gradually relaxed, until P.T. sessions commenced on the upper deck. Vaulting bucks appeared as if from nowhere and I even saw, for the first time, dummy bayonet fighting apparatus in action. Away, out of sight, went the restricting clothing of northern climes and out came shorts and singlets in their place, leading to a complete change in the ambience of life onboard. Suddenly, the world seemed to be a much brighter and more cheerful place, as sunshine and cool breezes replaced icy winds and raging seas, which had made our Northern 'runs' so difficult!

We gazed daily at the huge ships, sailing serenely on, so close at hand and thought of the men on board enjoying some respite from the toils and perils of war.

Tom Pepper had settled down quickly to life on board and went happily about his daily tasks with a smile and a cheerful word. It was great to see him recovered from his *Revenge* depression and enjoying life again. However, that blissful state was destined not to last very long, for, alas, poor Tom was the first casualty of the increasingly hot climate. He had not, unfortunately, been circumcised as a child and as he was, as we say politely, more than generously rigged in the marriage tackle department, which in his case was enormous and unusually shaped, rather like a cricket bat; he soon felt great discomfort in that region from the continual sweating, which no amount of washing could completely alleviate. Tom was suffering, so after little persuasion from his oppos, off he went to the Sick Bay for treatment and reassurance. The Medical Officer took one look at that mighty membrane and decided that here was a chance to make a name for himself in the medical world!

*Rodney* had a fully equipped operating theatre and, apparently, a circumcision had never been carried out aboard a R.N. vessel using a local anaesthetic. Here was the chance to achieve a glorious first in that field and poor Tom was the guinea pig!

We arrived in harbour and next day, when all was secure, a quivering Tom made his painful, reluctant way to the Sick Bay and operating theatre where the MO was eager to begin, what could be, his crowning achievement!

All went well and the offending tissue was removed and ceremoniously consigned to the waste bin. Next day, I went to visit my 'old buddy' and there, in a cot, he lay in all his mighty glory! The mutilated member was immersed in a 'tank' of melting Vaseline and very sorry for itself it looked! Tom was pale and obviously suffering, but I managed to cheer him up a bit, by reminding him what a formidable performer he would now be, with the encumbrance on his member's end finally removed, leaving him free to ravage at will!

Some weeks afterwards, the MO who couldn't wait to reveal his achievement to the unsuspecting world, convened a conference on board of all fleet Medical Officers, at which all would be revealed. Tom, recovered now, was summoned to the Sick Bay, where a medley of medics waited impatiently for the unveiling. Tom's name was called and in he went, somewhat apprehensively, to confront that august body.

'This is Tom Pepper', announced the MO, importantly, at which there was a clearing of throats and a shuffling of papers.

'Would you please lower your trousers and underwear', intoned the MO Tom duly obliged and from that coven of hardened professionals, medically speaking, there arose a gasp of admiration, quickly suppressed!

The MO had already explained the intricacies of the operation and now for the unveiling. He picked up a wooden pencil, leaned slowly forward, placed it gently under the object of their admiration and attempted to lift it! His wrist creaked, and he leaned forward to obtain a better purchase! There was a loud 'crack', and the over loaded pencil snapped! The medics, who had been craning forward to obtain a better view, jumped back apprehensively and Tom allowed himself a wry smile. The story soon spread around the ship and within hours, Tom found himself not only the hero of the hour, but a legend in his own lifetime!

'Bathrooms' on board at this time were a pretty basic provision and consisted of a fairly large compartment with a composite floor, a row of toilets along one side and wash basins along the opposite side. The toilets had no doors and merely a half partition dividing them. There was absolutely no privacy at all. In the evening, after coming off watch, or finishing work, we would gather up our dhobying gear and stroll along to the bathroom, where we would strip to the 'buff', fill the wash basin with hot water and commence washing our underwear, socks, or any other items to be cleaned. There were, of course, no washing powders, like Persil or Daz then, merely bars of 'Pussers Hard' soap, which we obtained on board.

I was the proud possessor of a tin, the sides of which I had perforated with many small holes, attached a piece of line to the top and deposited any odds and ends of soap inside. Holding the line clear, I 'dunked' the tin in the hot water, hopefully creating something of a lather, which made the whole dhobying operation much easier to perform.

Hammocks were laid flat on the deck and scrubbed with a stiff brush, as were duck suits, which we wore when attending school on board.

On completion, we would then proceed to wash our bodies, usually spinning a yarn with our 'oppo', or a messmate who happened to be present carrying out his own dhobying session.

Having been used to, for many years, being naked in a crowd, albeit made up of males only, I had no inhibitions about the naked body, and for me it was a natural state of affairs, which was just as well, considering a complete lack of privacy at all times.

Size of a 'privy member' was never a problem for any of us. Those lads who were 'blessed' were admired, it was true to say, and we had some good laughs on the subject when women were mentioned, but we usually christened the lucky owner, Horsey, Donkey, and we had no hang-ups about it, as many of today's feminists would like to believe. Feminists, I believe, are consumed by a fierce jealousy, because they are different to men, both physically and psychologically, and would like to believe that they are men's equal, but as every form of competition between sexes is heavily rigged in their favour, the 'poor darlins' are proved to be incapable of succeeding on their own merits. If imitation is indeed the sincerest form of flattery, we men should feel extremely flattered, for just look around and see the large numbers of women who wear men's clothing, adopt men's names, swear coarsely, drink pints of beer and generally behave in a way which they see as manly, all the time 'slagging off' the very men they are copying so assiduously!

The ship's company granted shore leave, landed at King Tom pier and proceeded to explore what was then a very primitive place. Native dug-out canoes came alongside their occupants clad only in a form of loincloth, with their native wares displayed hopefully about them. Carved figures, fruit, palmleaf fans and a generally poor quality of goods were to be had, but business was anything but brisk and no one was exactly rushing to buy.

Palm wine was the local 'hooch' and despite prior warnings, many lads succumbed to its potency and very much regretted their weakness. Boys' leave was severely restricted, as usual, but from accounts of those who did taste the rather dubious local 'delights', we didn't miss very much!

The loud cries of 'You jig-a-jig, lovely white school-teacher' usually led to some filthy hut with a mountain of black flesh, sprawled inside and anyone who sampled that 'schoolteacher' needed a very strong stomach, indeed, plus a lot of luck to keep clear of the VD ward in RNH Haslar.

Venereal disease, in those days, was treated very seriously and led first to all leave being stopped for the sufferer and removal to a special mess in isolation. Many times, moving around the country, I have encountered a secluded, little, rose covered cottage, which the proud owner has lovingly called, 'Rose Cottage' and have had a little smile to myself, for that indeed, is the nickname given by 'Jack' to the isolation mess provided for VD cases on board! When in harbour, these men had to muster at given intervals to ensure that they had not slipped quietly ashore, and checks on their whereabouts were strictly enforced at all times.

Malaria, prickly heat, dysentery and many other diseases abounded in Freetown and a tiny cut, if not quickly treated, would soon fester into a painful sore. I believe that we all suffered from prickly heat at some time or another, usually on the buttocks, where, however hygienic one would be, thousands of tiny prickly 'pimples' would appear and make life miserable, with their stinging, itching presence, as the interminable sweat ran down!

At last and not before time in my opinion, we sailed from Freetown on the long leg back to Liverpool or Iceland, wherever we may be needed to escort a convoy to safety. German raiders were loose in the Atlantic and many fine, virtually defenceless ships went to the bottom on encountering their superior fire-power. Submarines were of course the worst menace and small ships such as destroyers and corvettes performed a dangerous and arduous task in thwarting them, but if a pocket battleship, or heavy German cruiser appeared on the scene, only desperate measures by the smaller ships, could save the convoy, from a cruel face.

One day, steaming peacefully along, a lookout reported an object off the bow. Further inspection proved it to be a small, sailing boat steering an erratic course over the calm sea. A destroyer sped off to intercept the boat and moving in close, saw several figures slumped inside it, as though asleep. They were indeed in the sleep from which there is no awakening and had been adrift so long without food or water that their very bodies had become completely dehydrated and when touched, crumbled away to dust!

News of this tragedy had a cold sobering effect on all of us and we thought first of the relatives, far away, who waited fearfully for news of their loved ones, knowing full well that such news, when it came, could mean that they would gaze on that loved one no more!

We sailed into harbour at Gibraltar, the 'Rock', familiar to all matelots in those days and a really good, lively, run ashore. The main street was an endless row of bars with loud flamenco style music, duty-free booze and tantalising Spanish girls. Battleships, cruisers, destroyers and ships of all types and sizes packed the harbour. During the hours of darkness, boats patrolled the harbour, dropping small depth charges at intervals throughout the night in an attempt to discourage, or force to the surface, any midget submarines lurking beneath the waves, preparing an underwater attack on the ships lying alongside. The Italians were particular experts at this form of attack and at Alexandria, succeeded in disabling two British battleships at a crucial point in naval warfare in the Mediterranean war zone.

It was decided that to relieve the boredom of boys having to remain on board through leave restrictions, a tour of the tunnels and workings of the 'Rock' would be organised and this proved to be an 'interesting' experience for us in a way of which, I am sure, the 'powers that be' had never intended. We were met onshore by our 'guide' for the tour, who was a very tall, gaunt-looking man, looking rather like 'Count Dracula', but not as handsome. He introduced himself, gave a short description of what we should see on our trip and then we were off. The extent of tunnelling and excavation work carried out was truly amazing, from the long galleries, the hospital, living quarters, ammunition stores, to the gun emplacements. We were fascinated by it all and Tom and I trudged along, taking in the sights, chattering away and hardly noticing that several boys were fairly shooting past, at a rate of knots, making for the head of the file.

Suddenly, we did notice that we were near the rear of the line, so we speeded up the pace and catching another of the lads, asked what was going on and why the big hurry?

'Don't be last,' said the boy, 'Unless you want a long, bony finger up your 'jacksee'.'

All became crystal clear for the 'guide', hanging back to close the watertight door between each section as we passed through, took to helping the last boy on his way with afore-mentioned bony finger and hence the speedy movement of the lads! The tour did make a break from life on board, but I am sure that a quick check in the Guinness book of records would show it to have been the fastest ever carried out on foot! We returned to the comparative safety of life on board and its humdrum routine, but that night all hell broke loose. We had received urgent sailing orders, and many of the ship's company had celebrated too well, but not too wisely, on shore that evening. Eventually, all was sorted out and except for a parted six-inch hawser, which snaked viciously around the foc'sle, fortunately harming no-one, all was well and *Rodney* was under way again.

Our destination was the dreaded Scapa Flow, probably the most hated anchorage for shore-loving matelots ever! Bleak and desolate, swept by icy winds and with a low, featureless landscape, inhabited only by wandering sheep, or so it seemed, that was to be our barren Christmas billet.

There was shore leave, of a sort, with a cinema and a beer canteen, reached after a miserable journey in a drifter ashore. The canteen sold draft beer, but no money changed hands. At the entrance, we bought tickets, one for each pint we expected to drink and presented them at the bar, as and when required! The beer was strong, probably a crafty ploy to keep us quiet and subservient and I remember seeing actual hops floating in it. We poured it down our throats, without thought of tomorrow, just trying to forget the misery of the present and afterwards, back at the drifter, waiting for the journey back on board, fights broke out everywhere, as destroyer crews taunted 'big ships', forever swinging round a buoy on piles of cans dropped overboard during their long stay in harbour and we retaliated with great gusto!

All in 'good fun', for weren't we all the victims of this insane war which kept us from our homes and loved ones? Politicians made wars, and the ordinary people fought them and suffered. For what! A return to the 'old days' and the unfulfilled promises of better times ahead, that our fathers and grandfathers were placated with not so many years ago! Those who created war carried on in comparative luxury and safety and were the 'armchair heroes' of the future, while the so-called lower deck, went back to their ever present struggle to make 'ends meet' forgotten!

# CHAPTER SEVEN

*Reflections.*

We settled back into Harbour routine and I scuttled around the ship with yet more signals, finding my way around as though I had, as in the expression 'Son of a gun', actually been born on board. Officers with whom we came into contact continued to show their true character when in authority by indulging in their own little personal whims, because, of course, we were easy victims to their strange mood swings, primarily activated by them having not had a satisfactory evening meal, or even, in some cases, having attracted the disapproving eye of their senior officer after some minor mishap during the day. Possibly, the expensive wine at table was not sufficiently chilled, or some such major catastrophe had taken place!

We boys had to be turned in our hammocks, with gear stowed neatly, before evening rounds at 2100 reached our messdeck and never, during my time on board, in harbour, did we ever fail to meet this 'desirable' target, so, I have no idea what awful fate would have befallen us had we not done so.

It had happened, perchance, that we were among the first group of boys to be issued with pyjamas and one officer, when 'Officer of the Day' doing rounds, took it upon himself to make sure that we were indeed wearing them! As the party led by a Royal Marine bugler approached the messdeck, the duty Regulating Petty Officer, leading the officer of the day (probably to prevent him getting lost) sang out, in a loud, clear voice, 'Attention for rounds. Silence on the messdeck', at which, in a normal messdeck, everyone stood up and stopped talking, hoping the officer's eye wouldn't fall on them for some minor infringement of rules, but, on the boys' messdeck, we were required to 'lay to attention', bearing in mind that the O.O.D. couldn't see us and we couldn't see him beyond the high sides of the hammock. This particular 'bright spark' wasn't satisfied with that idiocy, but had to peep over the side of the hammock to make sure we were truly at attention!

Another of his favourite ploys was to order the R.P.O. to order everyone to 'turn out and stand by your hammock', simply to ensure that we were indeed wearing the aforementioned pyjamas, something which he obviously undertook as a personal crusade!

What a plonker and an example of the treatment meted out to lads who were volunteers and could have stayed 'safely in civvy street' for at least three more years!

At the end of W.W.II, experienced and battle-tested men left the Navy in droves causing a dreadful shortage of skilled men when the Korean War broke out and costing the country millions of pounds to lure back enough men to man the all too few ships we did send to serve the cause of the United Nations.

Many of those men, too, were the dregs of detention quarters and the 'scallywags' and troublemakers, selected by a trawl of the remains of Britain's once-mighty fleet, being practically 'pressed' into duty as a result of a swift 'pier-head' jump, as such methods were known in the Navy and once on board were denied shore leave, in case they took the opportunity to desert in double quick time!

I was still serving at that time in the newly formed Naval Police and as the youngest member of Town Patrol, Chatham, was the only member of that elite body not to have my service increased by an extra fourteen months as the only means of 'padding out' the remaining numbers of men in the Navy and to paper over the cracks that existed in the fabric of our fighting Services at that time.

After fourteen years' service, five of which were in wartime and two and-a-half years of which didn't even count toward Pension, or promotion rights, I was less than overwhelmed by their 'Lordship's' generosity in awarding me the less than princely sum of one hundred pounds gratuity, when those 'reluctant' warriors, were 'bribed' in the sum of one hundred and twenty five pounds, to return to the 'fold' for three years service!

The ingenuity of the lower deck matelots, at that time, in whiling away the long, boring hours and providing some form of 'entertainment' was truly amazing! Bearing in mind that much of the time, even in harbour, it was impossible to enjoy the delights of shore leave and unlike the other Services, recreational and entertainment facilities were difficult to come by. We had the usual spelling bees, quizzes and such like, but these pursuits were hardly electrifying entertainment. Uckers, draughts and chess were also popular with the more staid members of the ship's company, but there were those who sought to enliven the leisure hours in a much more unconventional and exciting manner!

One favourite 'sport' was cockroach racing which blossomed from being a good laugh to a fine art. Watch was kept around the ship for a likely candidate for the training stables and when such a thoroughbred was captured, he (or she) entered a life of sheer, sybarite luxury. Home for the 'pampered one' was usually an empty matchbox, or some such container, delicately lined by some horny-handed enthusiast with cotton wool or other soft material and stowed in a warm, dry spot under the eagle eyes of its minders. There were, sometimes, reports of unsporting attempts at 'nobbling' a fancied runner or established champion, so every precaution was taken to protect the 'Golden Hope'. The lucky creature was 'issued' with a daily 'tot' of rum and, of course, a successful champion would have 'sippers' or even 'gulpers' after winning, or defending the 'title'. Heats for the competition were a comparatively low key affair as the hopeful 'gallopers' of messes within a department battled it out. That winner would then race against other mess winners until a divisional champion was selected. Divisional 'champs' would then race until the semi and final were arrived at, which was when the excitement rose to fever pitch and bets would be laid and the various virtues of the competing champions be extolled around the ship.

Came the big night, and the course, in the main rec space was lovingly prepared and carefully marked out, under the scrutiny of watchful stewards and eager spectators. The big moment arrived and in a flurry of cheers and bobbling excitement, the contestants were introduced to the noisy crowd. Straight chalked lines marked the lanes of the course and the handlers carried their precious charges to the start line. Music played loudly, echoing the 'Entrance of the Gladiators' and the Senior Steward took up his important post! All was ready and an expectant hush fell over the sporting fraternity!

One blast of the Chief Steward's whistle and they were off, racing to the finishing line, driven on by the cheers or groans of the eager spectators until, with a deafening roar, the line was crossed and the race won! A babble of chatter broke out recounting the thrills of the race as the weary contestants were carefully and reverently gathered up and restored to the luxury of their padded boxes, then carried carefully to their sheltered resting place, for a last tot, before sinking gratefully to rest at the end of a tiring, exciting day, when a champion had been gloriously crowned or, sadly, defeated!

Another highlight of the sporting calendar was the 'Heinz' gooseberry contest, also carried out in the rec space and featuring even more highly trained contestants, who at the end of their 'ordeal' would be exhausted beyond relief! Heinz contest trainees relied on a daily diet of baked beans and such was the dedication to this 'sport' that there always arose a shortage of such delicacies, as those taking part cornered the market. The gooseberries were specially imported on board after a careful search to find that only those conforming to the rigorous requirements of the organisers were used on the big night.

There were many false starts and disasters on the run-up to the final in this competition and many who participated sadly qualified for an early bath, to the broken-hearted disappointment of their ardent supporters.

The night of nights was finally here and after the long and difficult trail to their pinnacle of achievement, the five finalists had a tired, wan look about them, the result, no doubt, of their long, difficult training. Now, however, all that was forgotten, in the excitement of the gala night and they stood, resolute and sturdy, clad only in a medley of varied-coloured dressing gowns, prepared to give their all for the honour of their department! There was a buzz of interest as the gooseberries arrived, carefully packed in a sturdy cool box and were inspected by the organisers in an unhurried professional manner. Size, firmness and quality of the gooseberries won universal approval and after a huddled conference, the contest was announced as 'Ready to begin'.

The contestants stepped forward and dropped their dressing gowns at their feet, standing in the 'buff', as it were and showing no apparent signs of competition nerves, which was just as well for those who stood closest. The fully dressed 'helpers' stepped forward and selected, carefully, a competition gooseberry from the gilded box. Competitors turned on the start line and leaning forward, placed a hand carefully on each of a second helpers shoulders and called in a firm voice, 'Ready, one; Ready two' and so on, till all had registered their readiness!

A single whistle blast was the signal for helpers to lean forward and place a gooseberry between the cheeks of the bum of their Great White Hope and then call, 'Ready'.

There was a second whistle blast, which was almost drowned by a thunderous roar from the rear of the five contestants and five perfectly balanced gooseberries flew through the air with rocket-like speed. Spectators staggered back, then swiftly recovered and cries of amazement and triumph rent the air. 'Big Jock' in number two lane had outstripped his colleagues by some three feet and now, pale and exhausted, was receiving the admiring congratulations of his helpers, when suddenly, there was an outcry and the word 'Cheat' filled the air!

What was this climax to what had been a night of clean, friendly sportsmanship? A helper of one of the competitors had retrieved the 'flying gooseberry' of the apparent winner and, on examining its glossy surface, declared loudly that it had been shaved thus giving 'Big Jock' an unfair advantage.

Spectators were stunned! Never in the long history of this famous competition had anyone taking part been even accused of cheating, but, after a hurried conference by the officials and a close examination of the offending gooseberry, the winner was pronounced 'disqualified' and the 'Heinz' crown awarded to a hairy stoker from five mess, who was formally declared 'The Winner'.

Boxing matches were also very popular and well attended. The usual inter-mess or divisional rivalry was exploited to the full as preparations for the contest proceeded and the day of reckoning drew near. I knew of one ex-pug, by then a bit 'punchy', who took part in many of these 'fights' and had two self-elected 'trainers' who convinced him that training should be a serious affair and that the daily tot was detrimental to their fighter's physical conditions so they did him a favour and from then on shared it between themselves to the considerable amusement of their messmates.

In Freetown one evening, a fight was billed as being between 'Punchy' and a local tribal chief, Massambula, to be held on the upper deck of *Rodney*. The ring was duly erected, strong lighting over the ring set up and, at last, all was ready for the clash of the 'giants'.

Sure enough, it the appointed time, a boat drew alongside from which emanated a blood-curdling roar like the savage sound of a wild beast at bay! Poor Punchy turned quite pale and stared anxiously toward the gangway. Under the dim gangway lights, a fearsome creature hove into view, roaring and rattling the chains that secured it to two burly, black figures, who themselves, looked as though they had come straight from some bestial, tribal, bloodletting orgy. The hairs on the back of my neck stood up sharply and I wasn't even in the ring, so imagine the look of sheer terror that came over Punchy's face as that apparition came near. The monster climbed with much roaring and howling into the ring, but someone had mercifully decided that enough was enough and as the referee called the contestants together in the centre of the ring, the monster was 'unveiled' and from under the 'beastly' makeup came forth the biggest electrician on board and poor Punchy could breathe freely again! The fights went on in the still, warm air and a great evening was had by all.

Back in Scapa, the boys had to attend school to prepare for an examination known as E.T.2, which, if we were successful, would qualify us educationally for uprating to Chief Petty Officer, so it was, of course, of great importance to us and our future in the Navy.

Papers were sent to the Admiralty for marking and assessment of ability, so results were not only important for us but for the reputation of the ship and her schoolmaster.

That over, we did a seaman torpedoman's course on board and at its conclusion, an examination and to my great satisfaction, I passed with a resounding eighty-five percentage pass mark, one of the best results. That was the end of school for me, but others, more ambitious, went on to take H.S.E. which qualified them, educationally, for officer rank. I had no illusions on that score. I was definitely not officer class and had I proceeded with my comrades and been successful, which is quite possible, would have been most unhappy in that artificial environment. Those who proceeded successfully to Wardroom rank worked hard and long, with the right training and the best naval background and deserved every success that came their way!

We prepared now for a Christmas at Scapa and like servicemen around the globe decided to make the best of it! At least we were warm and fed and had our 'oppos' around us, and my thoughts went out, at that time, to the thousands of men who were in dangerous and difficult situations, were wounded, or in grim P.O.W. camps! Yes, we had much to be thankful for that Christmas of 1941 and there were many more to come, which I would consider to be far worse.

Messes were gaily decorated (there was a competition for the best mess) and we even held a dance on Christmas Day in the main rec space, at which some extroverts dressed as women and pranced about in lively fashion. Of course, dance was a well-established form of exercise on naval ships, as anyone who read the Journal of Captain Bligh and his epic voyage in the Bounty would know and dancing the Hornpipe is still a 'must' at the Royal Tournament, annually, at Olympia.

One favourite Aunt had sent me a large cigar for Christmas and on the day I was determined to smoke it, even if it killed me, which it very nearly did. I apparently changed colours through the whole medium of the spectrum and then changed back again but, I did smoke it, despite not being much of a smoker at that time.

Some of the lads and I, had a run ashore to the beer canteen and sat there like real veterans, supping our beer and spinning yarns and enjoying a rare night out, but of course, nothing is for nothing in this harsh world, and next day we groaned as we moved and at every little sound, swearing 'never again'. Well, not till next time anyway!

The year 1941 was drawing to a close and, for the Navy, it had been a time of unmitigated disaster, with the loss of so many fine ships and, sadly, so many brave men. Pride of the Royal Navy, *HMS Hood* and all but three of her gallant ship's company had disappeared 'in a flash'. *Repulse* and the 'new' battleship, *Prince of Wales*, were lost after a desperate battle with overwhelming numbers of Japanese aircraft, the direct result of a stupid decision to sail, despite lack of air cover, by an Admiral who had always refused to acknowledge the deadly threat of modern attack aircraft, to the traditional role of outdated battleships. The debacle of Crete, where the Army fought so gallantly against superior forces and the Navy lost so much of its active fleet in the Mediterranean in an attempt to support them and eventually were forced to evacuate their defeated remnants.

*York*, *Bonaventure*, *Fiji*, *Gloucester*, *Greyhound*, *Kashmir* and *Kelly* sunk, many other ships badly damaged, and men lost simply because the Royal Air Force could not provide adequate air cover for our forces. Many a hoary, old ex-matelot grandfather would have been rocking his loving grandchildren on his knees today if the RAF had not been so sadly lacking in its support of not only our forces in Crete, but also during the long siege of Malta, which the Minister for Air, Sir Archibald Sinclair, decided would be indefensible should the

Axis forces attack the island and therefore failed to provide suitable air defences when that attack, foreseen by many, actually came, causing great damage and loss of life.

Later, the legendary aircraft carrier, Ark Royal, was torpedoed by U-81 off Gibraltar and sank, thus ending a long running saga of claim and counter claim by opposing Governments concerning its fate.

Loss of Hong Kong, which, with Singapore, was one of the Navy's most important bases in the Far East, and surrendered only after a bitter struggle, was also a bitter pill to swallow but, fortunately for our peace of mind, we were not aware that worse was to follow and we hoped that with the Americans in the war, after the Japanese surprise attack on Pearl Harbour, events would take a turn for the better and that a veritable flood of men and materials would pour across the Atlantic from the New World to aid the embattled people and forces of Great Britain! For the Royal Navy, there had never been a period of so-called 'Phoney War'. Our war had been real, from the very beginning and not many people realise that with war being declared on September 3rd, the British liner, Athenia, was sunk by U-30 off Ireland on September 4th and there was nothing 'phoney' about that horrific tragedy.

On Monday 18th September, the aircraft carrier *HMS Courageous* was torpedoed by U-29 with the loss of 515 lives! Nothing 'phoney' about that either!

On 29th December, 1941, I 'celebrated', if by any stretch of the imagination one could call it that, my seventeenth birthday, swinging round a buoy in Scapa Flow, just one of the many birthdays I would spend in different parts of the world for some time to come.

*Rodney* resumed her escort duties and about this time I became extremely glad to be at sea in a battleship and not one of the small escort vessels.

We steamed into a gale off Iceland, a notorious location for unpredictable weather conditions and this one was a real 'stinker' with forty-foot waves crashing down on to the upper deck with such tremendous force that a huge stanchion in the rec space supporting the upper deck buckled under the strain and the breakwaters athwart the upper deck forr'd were flattened.

Over the tannoy came a message that no-one was permitted on the upper deck, but the usual idiot decided to empty a 'gash' bucket over the side. As he stepped forth upon the upper deck a huge wave struck his helpless body and smashed it against the superstructure, fracturing his skull in the process.  As stated before, *Rodney* was fortunate to be equipped with a fully efficient operating theatre and the unfortunate rating was carried there.  On being examined it was decided that a special instrument would be required to carry out the necessary operation on his skull, but this 'tool' was not carried on board.  The engine-room artificers, some of the best trained at sea anywhere in the world, decided that they would manufacture the instrument which they proceeded to do at once.  The operation was a resounding success and the rating survived to reflect on the foolish act which so nearly cost him his life.

At times, corvettes steamed into a giant wave and disappeared and we watched with bated breath for them to re-surface and it seemed a veritable lifetime before they did so.

Back in harbour, we boys received our E.T.2 certificates from Admiralty, indicating that we had been successful in the exam, and as we concluded our seamanship training at sea, it was then simply a question of waiting for time to pass before being uprated to ordinary seaman and then to able seaman.  We would then have to qualify professionally for leading seaman and beyond but, with our extensive training, this was considered by those in authority to be a mere formality, if we managed to keep our 'noses clean' as the saying goes!

While in Iceland, about this time, we were paid a visit by Douglas Fairbanks Jr. who was serving in *USS Tuscaloosa* and, accompanied by a Lt. Commander RN, he proceeded to tour the ship, visiting the Boys' messdeck and expressing his surprise at our young ages.  I managed to obtain his autograph and was very impressed with his warm, friendly approach which contrasted sharply with that of our own officers.  He was leaving our mess and moving in to the electricians' next to ours, when a burly matelot, aggressively thrust his face forward and said, 'You're a good kid on the screen, but what can you do for real?'

Douglas Fairbanks, to his eternal credit, had his jacket off, one-one-two, before the Lt. Commander could blink even and offered to wrestle the oaf, there and then!  A minor scuffle ensued, before D.F. went on his way, smiling and completely unruffled.

Out of the blue came a signal that we were to proceed to Liverpool where *Rodney* would be fitted with additional armour for her upper deck and leave would be granted to both watches.  What excitement!

We boys could hardly contain ourselves and started preparing our kit right away!

At last the great day arrived, travel warrants were issued and we were off, on the long journey home to Dagenham. On my last leave visiting my Grandmother at Romford, she had presented me with a wristwatch as a good luck token and a farewell gift, but in the rush and excitement to be off, I forgot the watch and left it lying in my locker, which had on it a sturdy padlock, so I wasn't too worried about its safety.

My companion for the journey home was another Dagenham boy, Billy James, with whom I had become quite friendly on board and looked forward to enjoying his company during the leave period.

Billy's father had been a miner in Wales and when pits were closing and depression stalked the land, he moved with his family to Dagenham, as did thousands of others, to look for work at the Ford plant there and on being successful in his job hunting, decided to settle there for good. Billy was therefore of Welsh stock although his 'cockney' accent was more pronounced than mine ever was.

We arrived at my house in Canonsleigh Road first, but, despite nearly battering the door down, could get no reply, so, leaving my small attaché case in the porch, we repaired to Billy's house around the corner and after the excitement of homecoming had died down a bit, it was decided that I should sleep there and contact my folks in the morning. Worn out with eating, drinking and, of course, talking, we eventually went to bed and slept heavily till morning.

Meanwhile back at Canonsleigh Road my parents, who because of frequent air raids, slept in their comfortably equipped shelter every night, thus not hearing our 'door battering' exercise, had come to life and returned indoors and on opening the front door to pick up the milk, saw my case lying there. Panic ensued and Mum washed and dressed like a whirlwind and rushed to my Aunt's house in Goresbrook Road, thinking that I'd look for shelter there but, no son! Mum and Aunt Ethel then carried out a search of all the Public Shelters in the vicinity but to no avail! By this time, Billy and I had surfaced, and washed and dressed, were devouring a hearty breakfast. Thanking my hosts for their generous hospitality, I strolled round home and met the folks! For some strange reason, Mum always swore that her innocent young son had spent the night with a girl, probably making up for lost time and the more I protested my innocence, the more determined she became in her accusations, till eventually, I gave up trying to convince her. Thus are reputations made or destroyed and the innocent convicted!

I had a beautiful girlfriend, but she wasn't too happy about my long absences and my boozing with Billy, so it was a kind of on/off, relationship which was the kindest way to describe it.

Billy and I took two girls down the back of Heathway shops, where there was an entrance and exit road for shop deliveries. It was night time and he passed further down the road with his girl and I swiftly got down to work. Things were going really well and Ole Nobby was just about to make an entrance, when there came a thud and a scream from Billy's end of the road, followed by a clatter of running feet - Billy's!

'Quick, run,' he shouted and made off. I, with difficulty, disengaged my faithful friend, Nobby and hobbled off stiffly in Billy's direction and it was just as well that there was no pursuit, for I couldn't move very fast in my 'condition'.

'What happened?', I breathlessly queried Billy.

'She said no, so I thumped her', he replied!

Definitely not the act of a gentleman, I thought, not at all happy with such behaviour and the loss of such an act of 'love' at a critical point in the proceedings. Such is life, alas, full of disappointment!

Our ten days' leave was all too quickly over and we arrived back on board, tired and dejected after our long journey. The ship was in a state of absolute chaos and it was hard to believe that this scruffy mess was the immaculate *Rodney* we had left such a relatively short time ago! There was a gaping hole forr'd, connected to the dockside by a wobbly double plank gangway which the dockyard 'maties' used to enter and leave the ship and shortly after our return, a matelot under stoppage of leave decided to sneak ashore for a few pints using this 'gangway'.

Every morning the 'middy' of the watch would pace the upper deck scrutinising the dock bottom in case anyone had fallen overboard during the night. It was, by then, a routine inspection, probably quite boring, but on this instance necessary. He looked down and saw what appeared to be a bundle of rags lying far below and either being a conscientious young man, or wishing to break the boring routine, he decided to inspect the 'bundle' more closely and descended, carefully to the spot.

Huddled there, in the mud and slime, was the still breathing body of the 'absentee' matelot. He would 'scoff' no more pints, alas, for he died shortly after being moved, thus confirming the remark he made to a shipmate, just before creeping ashore 'I would die for a pint'!

Dockyard maties were everywhere and they had enjoyed a fine old time while we were away, apparently, for the lockers on our messdeck had been levered open, probably with a metal bar and a number of items were missing, including the watch Grandma had lovingly given me as a going away present, which was a real sickener!

There was a huge pile of dirty duffle coats on our messdeck collected prior to being cleaned by a shoreside laundry and one boy ran the length of the messdeck and with a loud 'yippee', jumped into the air and landed heavily on the duffle coats.

There issued forth a loud scream from the heap and a 'matey' staggered out, swearing mightily, with blood pouring from his nose and this was in the forenoon! We felt a little better after that incident, but the sense of loss felt at that time is still fresh in my memory.

There was a strike by stevedores around this time and a refrigerated ship carrying meat from Australia was marooned in the docks with no one to unload her! Volunteers were required from the ship's company to carry out that task and they rose to the occasion magnificently, with more than enough men coming forward. The job was done quickly and efficiently, and a few more hungry wartime bellies were filled as a result!

We matelots hated being in dockyard hands and now that leave was over, yearned to be away and for the ship to be restored to her former cleanliness and efficiency, without the dreaded maties tramping everywhere.

Additional anti-aircraft guns in the form of Oerlikon 20mm cannon were installed on the upper deck, which meant additional men to man them, which in turn, caused some problems with accommodation, but they were absorbed without too much difficulty into life on board, but it did mean that there was, in some messes, insufficient room for every member to sling their hammock. Mess stools were brought into use and some ratings slept on them, or spread their hammocks on the deck and, of course, when at sea, we were usually in two watches, four on and four off, which succeeded in alleviating the problem somewhat!

We proceeded to Iceland, back to the convoy routine and the icy wastes which I found to be a 'different' kind of cold when in harbour there. It was bitterly cold, but very dry at the same time and felt much healthier than the cold, extremely damp climate of Britain!

# CHAPTER EIGHT

*Malta convoys.*

Back in September 1941, *Rodney* had formed part of Force 'H' in company with the flagship and 'chummy' ship, *Nelson* (Admiral Somerville) the battleship *Prince of Wales* and aircraft carrier *Ark Royal*, with Force 'X', composed of four cruisers and nine destroyers (Rear Admiral H. Burrough) in an attempt to escort a convoy of nine merchant vessels through the Mediterranean from Gibraltar to re-supply the island of Malta, which was again in urgent need.

The Italian fleet once again put to sea, but soon steamed at speed back to the safety of its base at Naples, when a major fleet action seemed imminent. I remember clearly the storm of cheers that issued forth from *Rodney's* ship's company, when announcement was made over the tannoy that the Italian fleet was heading in our direction and the feeling of disappointment when they turned and ran for harbour.

The posturing and ranting of Benito Mussolini, the Italian dictator, and his boasts of his mighty, magnificent fleet made us all eager to put their quality to the test, but unfortunately, the Italian Navy were not at all keen on such a contest and when aircraft from Ark Royal made a torpedo attack on them, although low visibility made it unsuccessful, the nervous Italians showed a clean pair of heels and raced home!

Unfortunately, during an attack by torpedo carrying aircraft, *Nelson* was torpedoed right forr'd and her speed reduced to eighteen knots. One ship of the convoy, the Imperial Star, was sunk by aerial torpedo and sank, but the remaining ships reached Malta safely and the island could fight on. Operation Halberd was a success!

*Nelson* went into dry dock in Gibraltar and the Admiral and his staff were temporarily transferred to *Rodney*. An event occurred then of which I have never heard even a whisper and have never read in any of the many books written on the subject of war in the Mediterranean. A convoy was assembling off Gibraltar during the hours of daylight, which attracted some attention from those on board, as it appeared to steam aimlessly up and down, as though waiting instructions. One of the escorts was *HMS Cossack* of 'Altmark' fame and by the time the convoy sailed, the enemy had had sufficient time to give leave to its U-boat crews and still be in position lying in wait for them. Apparently, a near massacre occurred and many ships were lost, including *Cossack*.

Next morning, on board *Rodney*, a messenger proceeded to the Chief Of Staff's cabin with his usual morning call. He knocked, but there was no reply, so he carried on knocking! Still no reply! He then became worried and reported to the Officer of the Watch, who himself, attempted to rouse the C.O.S., but to no avail. Eventually, a shipwright was called to the scene and the door was removed. Behind it hung the body of the unfortunate officer, dead!

Stories flew round the ship like wildfire, but no official reference to the tragic incident was made then, or has been made since and the mystery lives on in my memory and possibly in the memory of many other men who were on board at that time. That *Cossack* was involved, I am doubly sure, for one of the survivors, Boy Swann, who served at *HMS St. George* with me, in 274. A.C. Class, was brought on board *Rodney* into the boys' mess, where we kitted him out as best possible with our own 'gear' and listened to his story of the action with, at first, disbelief and then with some dismay!

The next Malta convoy was an entirely different story and has been portrayed on film and in many books, so I will not go into great detail. Suffice to say that the action is considered by Naval history experts to have been the most hard-fought convoy battle of the war and despite the powerful escorting force, only five of the fourteen original merchant ships reached Malta and they were all damaged in some way or another. The single most important vessel, the tanker Ohio, with its precious cargo of fuel oil and kerosene, 10,000 tons of which arrived safely, despite the dreadful battering both the ship and her ship's company had received during that traumatic, epic journey, was virtually coaxed into Malta, under tow and the efforts of the R.N. ships that made her arrival possible. Penn, Rye, Bramham and Ledbury, with minesweepers, Speedy, Hebe and Hythe, should be written high in the annals of Naval history as a shining example to future generations of young Navy men of what can be achieved, against formidable odds, by sheer determination, by skilled inventive seamanship and a grim dedication to duty!

Operation 'Pedestal' too was a success, for in spite of dreadful losses, in both men and ships, Malta was saved and their sacrifice was not in vain! Little did I or my comrades imagine that some fifty years later, we would be guests at the Palace, Valetta and the President of

Malta, Dr. Censu Tabone, who himself worked as a doctor in Malta during the siege, would present us, personally, with the Malta Commemorative Medal, in recognition of service rendered to Malta during those turbulent days! The people of Malta, did not forget!

*Rodney* returned to Scapa Flow and to my great delight, I was promoted to Ordinary Seaman, at seventeen years and six months of age, which was recorded on my Service Certificate as 'Specially Rated' and was indeed a reward for all the years of service that had gone before. This meant, in turn, that my days of sea training were over and I rapidly received a 'draft chit' back to my home depot, *HMS Pembroke*, Chatham, Kent, and shortly afterwards a group of some ten ratings, some returning for courses, some on promotion, left *Rodney* for the last time and started on the long journey from Scapa to Chatham and though I did not know it at the time, a move which would change the whole course of my service career and finally, as a result of that change, lead to disillusionment with the Navy and a fervent desire to escape from its restricting clutches. Billy James was one of the party travelling to Chatham and another member was an Able Seaman, whom I knew slightly on board and had a well-deserved reputation as a lower deck lawyer, so when he suggested that on arrival we should proceed as a party, just in from sea, which immediately qualified us for ten days 'in from sea' leave and that we let him do the talking in his skilled tongue, we readily agreed.

The fact that we had recently enjoyed ten days' leave was not to be mentioned and as it was not entered in our paybooks, ensured that no-one would know that fact. Sure enough on arrival we reported en masse at the leave office, and to our surprise, were all granted ten days' leave, so depositing our bags and hammocks in store, off we went, rejoicing, on our way! Billy and I boarded the bus to Gravesend, embarked on the ferry for the short journey across the Thames to Tilbury, but, on enquiring the time of the train to Dagenham Dock, were informed that we had just missed one. There was a licensed restaurant on the station approach, so Billy and I repaired there to alleviate the long wait with some liquid refreshment, which we proceeded to do with great gusto! By the time the train arrived, we were well away and, on arrival at Dagenham Dock virtually poured ourselves on to the platform and staggered off to the nearest pub, The Roundhouse, where we ordered more drinks. The

'Guvnor' refused to sell us a drink, but as we were matelots, gave us a pint each then steered us on our merry way.

We finished up at the Ship and Shovel just across the road from my home in Canonsleigh Road, where we proceeded to make merry, aided and abetted by the warm, friendly people of Dagenham, the greatest people on earth, as I told my enthralled audience later, whilst standing on a table. Reeling to the floor on the premise that I couldn't fall any further, I then passed out and commenced to snore my head off!

The pub 'audience', who, at that stage didn't know who the hell we were, or where we lived, had enjoyed the episode so much that they decided to take us home, personally!

Spotting our paybooks, which were hung round our necks in those days, they looked inside and were pleased to note how close to the pub I lived and that Billy's home was just around the corner, so they entered into the spirit of the thing and clutching an arm and a leg each, they set off for home, a laughing, cheering mob!

On arriving at No 6, they hammered mightily on the front door and apparently, Mum and Dad thought the long feared invasion had started and rose up in some fear to face the roaring crowd!

'What is it?' cried Mum, in a quivering, quavering voice.

'It's your son,' the crowd roared back, happy at bringing such good news!

'It can't be,' replied Mum, bewildered, 'he's away at sea!'

'O yes, it is,' they cried, in the approved pantomime fashion, so Mum gingerly opened the door, with Dad standing by, looking suitably fierce! 'My God', Mum cried, 'it is him, Ern,' and opened the door wide. With a quick, one, two, three, heave, my 'bearers' heaved me half way along the passage and with a final loud cheer and 'goodnight', off they went happily, their 'job' well done!

Next day, I was bruised from top to bottom and felt like death, but the family rallied round and carefully nursed me back to health. Five days later, thoroughly chastened, I stiffly walked round to see Lily, but when, being an honest lad, I eventually told her that I'd been home five days before seeing her, she exploded and saying, tearfully, that she loved me, but that I was a drunkard and irresponsible etc., and there was no future for us together. She bade me, in no uncertain terms to begone, so off I trudged, unhappily and decided that females were unreasonable creatures, with no sense of humour!

Now Dad, who was very strict with us boys, would not allow me to smoke in the house or in his presence, although I was in the Navy and serving at sea! Drinking alcohol for me was definitely taboo in his eyes and on my previous leave, with Dad either at work or fire-watching, I could get away with it, but now, all was revealed and I awaited his reaction with some trepidation.

When not working, Dad used to walk over to the Ship and Shovel on a Sunday and drink his pint quietly, just listening to the conversation and taking no part in it, so consequently, although he had been drinking there for some time, no one really knew him and he passed in or out unnoticed. When Sunday came, he cornered me and I thought, 'This is it!' But in his usual restrained manner he said, 'Now that it's obvious that you do drink, how about coming to the pub with me for a noggin?' I nearly collapsed with the shock of it, but managed to stammer an acceptance and away we went!

On entering, it seemed that most of the crowd were there from my 'debut' night and friendly greetings came from all directions. Cries of 'Hello there Jack, how's the head?' and, 'Has Mum got over it yet'? rang out and there I was, the centre of attention, with Dad smiling quietly in the background!

That one drunken 'binge' had convinced Dad that I was old enough to enjoy the sins of the flesh and that with age and maturity, I would find my own way and never again did he seek to impose his Victorian ideas upon my own somewhat wayward lifestyle. I cannot, in all honesty, say that he approved, but he knew now that his objections would cut no ice with me and, anyway, I would soon be beyond his control sailing forth on the briny!

Our leave was all too soon over and there were more 'goodbyes' and off we went back to Chatham, where I spent boring weeks of just walking about, trying to dodge the many eager barracks staff, who at the slightest opportunity, detailed off unwary sailors for an even more boring job. We slept then, because of the fear of air raids, in the tunnel which was literally just that and this meant having to carry the hammock from the block along the terrace to the tunnel where a billet had to be found in order to sleep (fitfully in my case) and then the whole miserable business had to be endured, in reverse, back to the block next morning! My efforts at dodging work paid off for a while, but either I became careless or someone noticed my wanderings around the barracks, for one day, my name was broadcast over the tannoy, directing me to report to the main office. On arrival there, I was detailed off to report to the 3-inch gun battery and there found that I was a member of the guns crew, watchkeeping, forty-eight hours about. Now this was a bit of good luck beyond belief, for when off duty, we slept in a special mess in St. Mary's barracks, separate from the main buildings and no more humping gear up and down to the tunnel, thank God!

On duty we lounged about the gunsite, or flopped out inside the shelter provided for our exclusive use. Some people played cards, some read books or newspapers, whilst others dozed or simply listened to the sometimes stimulating conversation that emanated from the card players. One day the red alert sounded and our gallant crew went bravely in to action. I was an ammunition number working between the locker and gun keeping the guns crew supplied with projectiles. The gun and the ammo were of World War I vintage and I had a tremendous shock when heaving away at the brass cylinder, it came away in my hands, leaving the projectile behind in the locker. Suddenly, I realised that the gun was more of a menace to us, the crews, than it could ever be to the enemy and some of the shine went off the job, right then and there!

Another day, we were off duty in the block when the alarm went, so we dutifully 'dropped everything' and galloped off at speed in the direction of the gun, as we were required to do. Flying along in my heavy boots, I suddenly encountered a Chief Gunner's Mate, lying full length in the gutter shouting his head off, 'Take cover, take cover' and alternately blowing loudly on a whistle, with all the lung power associated with men of his ilk. Somehow, I resisted the temptation to trample all over him and flew ever onwards, sadly realising that such a golden opportunity would probably never occur again in my lifetime! Chief and gunner's mates, or 'Gate and Gaiters', as they were sometimes called politely, were born with mouths like the entrance to Blackwall Tunnel and spent their entire days making life miserable for all junior ratings, whilst strutting about like clones of the Italian Dictator, Benito Mussolini and were generally the most hated men on the lower deck, until Leading Patrolmen 'happened' along and relieved them of that 'distinction'.

Barracks life, then, was sheer hell for seagoing sailors, in between ships and seemed designed to make life as uncomfortable and wretched as possible for those who deserved some rest and recreation after the very real rigours of life at sea in wartime. I have heard of some senior rates who spent the entire war years in the relative safety and comfort of their quarters, in barracks, and were too ready to behave as though they were the ones who suffered hardship by being there. Some were even decorated for such 'service' and, of course, were after the war the very ones who displayed their BEM as though it were really earned, whilst the men who saw action, generally, were not even recognised. Officers were another 'breed' who came into this category. Some deserved their award having, in a position of responsibility taken a decision which could have had some far reaching result either on the future conduct of the war, or on the lives and safety of their men, but others were given the award in recognition of a gallant action by a ship's company, or a group of which they were in charge and they usually prefaced their acceptance speech with phrases like, 'I accept this award on behalf of the men who served with me, without whom the success of the operation would not have been possible' and then proceeded to trade on it for the rest of their lives, whilst the men who made it possible had nothing to show for their gallantry in action!

The road at the barracks' entrance was lined with trees, which of course, shed their leaves annually. A permanent squad of matelots, complete with brooms, paraded all day virtually catching each leaf before it touched this hallowed ground, which was also patrolled by the so-called barrack guard, clad in belt and gaiters and carrying a whistle and woe betide any unsuspecting matelot who trespassed on the pavement either side of that road, a most heinous offence, which was met by whistle-blowing, shouting 'stooges', trained to do the work of their masters and force members of the lower deck to walk in the road, where, according to those 'masters', they obviously belonged!

Better by far that the ratings should be mown down by a passing car (Officers only) than that he should tread the same pavement as his lordly superiors!

Along the terrace stood the blocks which accommodated the ratings, each named after an Admiral of some bygone age. Nelson, Anson, Blake, etc., and each displayed a carved, highly painted figurehead representing that particular long-dead hero. I remember the 'Nelson' figurehead which had an arm, complete with long finger, pointing forward over the parade ground beyond the terrace, and on rounds day, which was every Saturday forenoon, messes were scrubbed out and tidied ready for inspection by a senior officer. Each mess had a bucket, known as the 'gash' bucket, in which the remainder of meals or any general rubbish generated in the mess was deposited. The problem was what to do with said bucket during rounds when the mess had to be nothing short of immaculate. Some members dodged ahead of the rounds party, circled around cleverly and returned to the mess when safe to do so, but one wag was not satisfied with such a mundane performance and dangled the bucket from Admiral Nelson's pointed finger, to the horror and dismay of the 'distinguished' members of the rounds party! This display of lower deck disrespect sent shock waves of alarm throughout the Wardroom and should the perpetrator of this near mutinous act have been discovered, he would probably have been shot at dawn, every day, for a week!

The perpetrator was not discovered and he, or a copycat, played a game of cat and mouse with the authorities, till eventually, they admitted defeat and ordered the offending member to be sawn off!

Life continued in a pleasant enough vein, with plenty of sleep, an occasional dash to the gun, fire a few rounds, then back to the shelter and dream the time away, until either the next alarm, or end of the watch came. Sometimes I decided on a quick dash to Dagenham for night leave, but it just wasn't worth all the hassle of catching bus, ferry, train and bus again, for a few hours at home, then a quick 'kip' and an early rising next morning to catch the 0615 train from Dagenham Dock station. On arrival at Tilbury station, another frantic dash to the ferry and reaching the Gravesend side, a sprint to the bus station at Overcliffe Depot, when at least, one did enjoy a bit of a rest, till arriving at Pembroke Barracks.

The trouble was the whole journey hinged on catching transport at each stage and a 'miss' at any one meant being adrift at Chatham and subsequently, punishment, i.e. stoppage of leave and pay and all the hassle that went with it. Even a minor offence in those days was treated as though the unfortunate offender had placed the very future of the Royal Navy at risk and the rating concerned would never be allowed to forget his lapse from the straight and narrow. Consequently, everyone undertaking the journey raced from place to place as though their very lives depended on being first on or off the transport. This had some unfortunate consequences for the railway staff at Tilbury, especially for the early morning ticket collector, who having no barrier as such, endeavoured to check the matelots' tickets as they hurtled past him.

Now, some of those matelots, not quite as honest as their colleagues, either couldn't afford the fare (after all, we were poorly paid in those far-off days) or had no intention of parting with their hard-earned cash, so they cut a rectangular shape, about the size of a ticket, from an empty Woodbine packet, which was roughly the same colour. They then dashed past the unfortunate collector, flashing the 'ticket' and before he could examine it closely, vanished on to the ferry. This ploy worked for some time, but one morning we were confronted at Tilbury by a sturdy wire barrier from floor to ceiling and a grinning collector who obviously thought that at last he had won what had been, till then, an unequal contest, but he had reckoned without the determination of 'Jack ashore' and he stood in the narrow gap still open, smiling, as the mob bore down on him, when he realised, too late, his foolishness. The 'lads' swept on, carrying all before them, including the collector, who found, suddenly, that an unexpected trip on the Gravesend ferry was imminent and there was nothing he could do about it!

The outcome of this incident was that several mornings later, a member of the Railway Constabulary stood sturdily in support of the collector, but he proved to be more intelligent than most of his ilk and on seeing the galloping mob approaching at full speed, decided that discretion was better than valour in this situation and stood gracefully aside as they thundered on their way, thus he survived to live another day!

About this time, there was a sneak air raid on the Dockyard, the aircraft dropping one bomb before fleeing! With all the valuable targets that were at hand, including ships, workshops and men, the pilot committed the unforgivable sin and bombed a 'maties' toilet, thus, instead of stealing a crafty, mid-morning smoke, the occupants were suddenly propelled on the journey from which there is no return!

I feel sure that one of our more educated 'scribblers' could find a meaningful lesson hidden somewhere in that unfortunate incident!

# CHAPTER NINE

*Combined operations.*
Early one day, the inevitable happened and my cosy little world was shattered, yet again. Over the tannoy came the pipe, 'Ordinary Seaman A. E. Garrod report to the Main Drafting Office, immediately.' There was the usual 'cheer' from my comrades around the gun and off I went, wondering what 'rust bucket' I would finish up on now!

'Draft chit, lad', said the three-badge leading seaman seated behind the office window, 'but don't ask me what kind of ship it is, for I've never heard of it'. The name is *Brontosaurus*, he said, 'and it's somewhere in Scotland'.

'Sounds pretty old', I quipped feebly, thinking to myself that it sounded like a minesweeper, which was probably based in some grotty little port in the wilds, and feeling not very happy at the mere thought of it. I was right with the grotty bit, but wrong on every other count! Next day I was off, alone, complete with the usual bag and hammock, on the long train journey to Dunoon, Scotland where, after a journey that seemed to take forever, I was met at the railway station by a friendly Wren, whose name I later found to be 'Betty', who welcomed me to *Brontosaurus*, which was no minesweeper after all, but a training camp for future landing craft crews, hidden in dank, murky woods, some seven miles from Dunoon.

This was worse than my worst thoughts come true and the start of one of the most miserable periods of my Service life.

Betty chatted brightly during the drive to the camp and I observed one ray of sunshine through the dark clouds ahead. At least there was crumpet in the camp. She explained that she drove the lorry which was the camp transport, but didn't live in the camp, but had a billet elsewhere. There were some ATS girls actually stationed there, but not many in number. At least, I thought, that was something!

On arrival at *HMS Brontosaurus*, my heart sank to the level of my boots and even tried to go further! The 'camp' was a collection of Nisson huts, erected on concrete bases and that appeared to be that!

On reporting to the Office, I was directed to No 5 hut and proceeded to plough through the mud with bag and hammock to reach it. The interior was heated (this was November) by a single coal, or woodburning stove in the centre and I was lucky to find a bunk fairly close to it. The top of said stove was red hot, but the temperature was definitely chilly! I settled in and was informed that the rest of the lads were down at the jetty where the landing craft were secured, so I had a 'shufti' round to get my bearings and found the dining hall, another Nisson hut, which felt even more chilly than the one I'd just left.

When the lads returned about 1600hrs, they greeted me like a long lost brother, which simply convinced me how desperate they were to see a 'new' face, as though they had been marooned on a desert island for years. They were a friendly lot and when I asked about the crumpet available, they simply laughed, or looked mysterious and said, 'Wait and see!'

The daily routine was simple enough. Rise at 0630, wash, tidy up the hut and then breakfast. After that, fall in on the parade ground (funny how they are always present, even if the comforts of life are absent) and then march to the jetty, carrying the day's meals in 'straw boxes' and there practice landings all day, or as an item of light relief, teach soldiers how to get in and out of a hammock on board the landing craft.

That was the really enjoyable bit, despite the cold, miserable weather and appalling food, which was definitely the worst I had encountered in my career so far! The soldiers, or 'pongoes', as we called them, were I believe part of the reconstituted 51$^{st}$ Highland Division that suffered dreadful casualties covering the retreat and evacuation at Dunkirk and they were a laugh a minute, especially when attempting to master the mysteries of climbing in or out of the hammock and, but for their innate cheerfulness and masterly control of the Scottish language (mostly swear words) the whole operation would have been miserable beyond description.

Many of them were short, wiry, little men, but what they lacked in height, they more than made up for in sheer guts and I would have been proud to have served with them anywhere!

They boarded the tank landing craft at the jetty and off we sailed over the Clyde to accustom them to the motion of the craft, when under way and then, turning, we made a dash for the beach, dropped the ramp and away they went, yelling and screaming up the beach. I don't know what they did to the enemy, but they sure scared the living daylights out of yours truly!

I was itching to meet the ATS 'girls', for after a couple of weeks of this camp, I would have ravished a gargoyle had one been available, out in this wilderness and I still hadn't seen the mysterious crumpet! When they did appear, after one look, I fancied the gargoyle even more! Instead of the 'Miss World Contest', the powers that be had obviously organised a 'Miss Ugly' contest and we had the 1$^{st}$, 2$^{nd}$ and 3$^{rd}$ 'winners'. I first thought the lads had cooked up a gag and persuaded three 'pongoes' to dress up in drag, but no, they were real, or as real as anyone that ugly could be!

Dressed in their drab, khaki uniform, which wouldn't exactly enhance any woman's appearance and with their faces quite heavily made-up, which had made me think they were men in drag, they were shapeless and one even had the legs of some hard-riding cowboy and couldn't have stopped the proverbial pig in a passage. The only point of any interest about them was that they, all three, sported a 'beauty' spot (on them, a complete misnomer) which daily they placed in a different position on their painted faces, so unfortunately we had to look at the face to 'spot the spot', as it were, which was a ghastly experience to say the least!

An officer who took command of the daily parade must also have been drafted to this isolated spot to hide him away, for he stuttered really badly when shouting orders and at first, I had such difficulty in not laughing each morning when he performed, that I almost burst a blood vessel with the effort!

When he shouted 'Parade, attention', he would manage the 'atten' bit, in fine style, but there he stuck and stuttered away fiercely! With one leg on the ground and the other permanently poised in mid-air, we waited expectantly for the finale and just as we started to feel the onset of cramp in the hanging leg, he would suddenly bark 'Shun', which took us all by surprise and there was a positive clatter of right legs falling to earth. At this, he would furiously but clearly shout, 'As you were' and we would hilariously go through the whole procedure again until he was satisfied! This performance soon began to pall and we fervently hoped that he would one day do us all a favour and fall overboard from the craft and vanish from our sight, probably stuttering as he departed elsewhere! I swear that when I left the camp, my left leg was twice the thickness of the right, which had simply wasted away through just hanging limply in the cold, damp air every morning!

Of course, with experience, we would later realise that only the decent, bother-nobody people fall overboard, or get sick and die and the pests and bastards of this world, go on forever, being themselves! In March 1942, Lord Louis Mountbatten, at the age of forty-one, was promoted by Winston Churchill to be Chief of Combined Operations and on 28<sup>th</sup> March 1942, Dieppe, the biggest Combined Operation of the war, so far was carried out. From this raid, many valuable lessons of the problems involved in this type of operation were learned and put to good use in the many raids and landings that took place later. Lord Louis decided to visit Combined Operations training establishments in Scotland and accordingly, a signal arrived warning the powers that be of his impending inspection of *HMS Brontosaurus*! There was not much that could be done to improve the appearance of the camp and with the incessant rain, it was clearly impossible to paint the grass green, any available stones white, or carry out any of the stupid 'facelift' procedures, of which many Naval officers were so fond, so we simply tidied the huts with a little more care than usual on 'the' day and fell in, wearing seaboots and oilskins, to await the arrival of the 'great man'.

Two hours after the appointed time, by which time we were cold, wet and were calling him (under our breath, of course) anything but his given name, he finally arrived. There was, naturally, no Royal Marine Band, or any other kind of band available and as we were called to attention (fortunately, not by the stutterer) he walked down the assembled ranks, shielded by an enormous umbrella, carried by one of his acolytes. He paused in front of my dripping figure and addressed me in a firm voice! 'And how old are you, lad'?

'Seventeen, Sir', I replied, equally firmly (I hoped).

Turning to his aide, he said, 'My God, they're getting younger every day!' then moved on, stopping at the next but one rating to me.

'Are we going to win?' he said, with a friendly smile!

But 'Jack', obviously 'chokka' with the long wait and appalling conditions, was having none of it and to everyone's astonishment, replied loudly, 'I've got my doubts, Sir'.

There was a stunned silence, broken only by an officer shouting, furiously, 'Get that man out of here'.

Get him out they did and by lunchtime he, complete with bag and hammock, had been whisked away back to civilisation, or at least, back to his old unit, never to be seen by us again!

So much for truth and honesty, a luxury not catered for in the Services. The talk back in the hut was of that daring young man who told Lord Louis and his 'merry men' exactly what they did not want to hear, but of course, he escaped from this 'dump' and we were still here regardless! Soon, Christmas time was upon us and there was no prospect of home leave to cheer our miserable existence. I tried hard to think of those unfortunates who were much worse off and who were really suffering severe hardship, but even such thoughts failed to lift the atmosphere of gloom which pervaded the camp.

Nearby was Castle Toward which we understood was owned by a rich woman, widow of a textile magnate, who also owned the land on which the camp stood. Volunteers were required to cut down and transport through the woods a large Christmas tree, which would enhance the festivities due to take place in the castle in a few days' time. We thought, in our ignorance, that maybe a drink, a mince pie, or perhaps even a warm evening at the castle fire might be the reward for our exertions, but after all the effort our high hopes were shattered by a quick, 'Thank you, return to camp', at the end of it. So much for the Christmas spirit and 'Goodwill to all men', but that sentiment obviously did not include the ratings, for the officers were invited and spent part, at least, of their Christmas in the comfort and luxury of its warm interior, while we shivered in the bleak misery of our Nisson hut!

One thing I do remember from that most miserable occasion was the popularity of Bing Crosby singing his hit song, 'I'm dreaming of a White Christmas' and when I hear the song, even today, I think to myself that was no dream, but a nightmare and a damp chill creeps over me at the very remembrance of it!

All good things come to an end and fortunately, so do the bad things. We had completed the course and were off once more into the unknown. It was pack bag and hammock time and this time I did it gladly, anxious to be off.

Into the lorry went our gear, then we piled in, to start another long journey from Dunoon Railway Station to RAF Calshot near Southampton, where we would be accommodated until our next posting was decided upon. Our arrival at the camp was like an entrance into another world. We were about twenty in number and had a hut to ourselves, but what luxury compared with our previous 'dwelling place'. It was warm, self-contained with toilets and washplace with plenty of hot water at all times. There was also a warm, clean, well-equipped dining hall and surprise, surprise, loads of gorgeous WAAFs. roaming about freely. Heaven! In the Navy, a leading seaman in charge of a mess of usually twenty men ate, slept and generally lived in the mess as one of the men, but here, when he sat at our table in the dining hall, he was promptly told that he must sit separately, as befitted his superior rating, which pleased him not at all.

After several shocked RAF 'bodies' had remonstrated with him unsuccessfully, he dismissed them with, 'Here I am and here I stay, with my men' and that was the end of that!

We had no duties and could walk out of the camp at appropriate times as did the RAF personnel and just outside the gates, in a small bungalow, lived two old ladies who devoted themselves to looking after the welfare of we poor young lads, torn from our loved ones by this wicked war! The ladies were wonderful and baked cakes incessantly, made platefuls of delicious sandwiches and made sure that a piping hot 'cuppa' was always available. They would fuss around us in a gentle, kind, motherly fashion and if anyone looked unhappy, they would chat comfortingly to them so brightly that no one could be miserable in their vicinity.

The debt we owed to those wonderful ladies cannot be expressed in mere words, but I am sure that when they appeared at the 'pearly gates', St. Peter will have organised a very special welcome for them!

A NAAFI wagon arrived outside the gates each day with the usual mixture of teas, cakes and sweets and we couldn't remember having lived in such comfort and having been so well fed in all our Service life. I promptly decided that if the Buddhists were right and we did return after death to another life on earth, given the choice I would definitely return as a member of the RAF!

On board ship, one was completely isolated from civilian life and the amenities available were obviously not to be compared with those enjoyed by personnel in British Army or RAF camps, where the sports facilities, accommodation and catering were of a much higher standard. At RAF Calshot, the very ambience of the camp was completely different, without the shouting and harassment of junior personnel, which was a common factor of Naval barracks life and men (and women) were treated like human beings and not like some species of sub-human animal.

We enjoyed a life of ease and luxury at 'Calshot' for about a week, then once again, we were on the move to another unknown destination. We were grateful for our period there during which we did our dhobying, luxuriated in a full length bath and I even bought a new pair of bootlaces to replace the ones that had rotted in the dampness of our previous environment. Everyone in the camp with whom we came in contact was kind and helpful toward us and did, indeed, restore some of my lost faith in human nature! Thank you, RAF Calshot!

Our next billet, proved to be a bit of a mystery! Why were we there and what was the point of our visit?

The 'billet' was a deserted radio station, surrounded by a high screen of barbed wire. There were no cooking facilities, we spread our hammocks on the bare floor but, fortunately, toilets and hot water were plentiful. Food was delivered daily by lorry, ready cooked and actually was not too bad, both in quality and quantity, so we simply settled in and hoped for the best which, from a practical point of view was all we really could do! This stay was a short one and after a couple of days, a lorry arrived and we were told to pack our gear and prepare to move!

We travelled for some time, wondering where the hell we would finish up this time as we passed through a forest, which someone remarked was the New Forest, Hampshire and that information made us even more puzzled. Finally, the lorry slowed and turned into a long drive, at the head of which we could see what appeared to be a stately home, next to which was a cluster of lower buildings, which proved to be our ultimate destination. We were comfortably ensconced in what was originally the servants quarters, which were fully equipped with bathrooms and bedrooms and fitted with Army style single beds.

A large room was used as a dining-hall, but I don't remember ever seeing who cooked the food and where it was cooked, but they sure made a good job of it, for which we were truly thankful!

Our 'dream' billet really was a stately home, that of Lionel de Rothschild of the family of international bankers, but commandeered by the Ministry of Defence as a secret planning centre where plans for the invasion of Europe were drawn up amid tight security. Our job was to guard it particularly from attack by enemy parachutists, which was considered to be an ever-present threat at that time. There was a sentry box at the entrance to the drive, another half way to the house and one in front of the actual house. We kept watch only at night when all three boxes were manned. A Petty Officer supervised us guards and made sure we performed our duties promptly and properly. We worked first, middle and morning watches, only and when off duty could go our own way, which included wandering around the incredibly beautiful grounds which we did with great pleasure. Being a London 'boy' who felt completely lost away from the pavements and vibrant noises of the 'city', it was a tremendous culture shock to find myself in such a place and to be allowed to wander at will through its 250 acres of woodland garden with its collection of rhododendrons, azaleas, camellias, magnolias and many fine shrubs and trees. I had no idea previously that people actually lived in such peaceful, exotic surroundings and when I gazed upon the tennis courts with their own refreshment bar, with their nets still hung, as though the players had merely paused for refreshment and would shortly return, I felt that this must be, indeed, the heaven to which the Bible referred!

*Paradise lost.*

An airborne attack on Exbury House at that time could have had but one tragic consequence for us all. Utter annihilation for the defenders and the easiest of victories for the attackers. Picture the scenario, if you will: Six young lads on duty, of whom I, the youngest, was the only one with any kind of military training, armed with World War I Lee-Enfield rifles and bayonet, with NO ammunition, against a German elite force, already toughened in combat in Norway, Belgium and Holland and armed with machine pistols, grenades and automatic weapons and with no possible idea that such a sensitive target would have such a 'ragbag' scattering of defenders. Fortunately they did not attack for which, to this day, I am truly thankful!

The middle watch was made nightmarish, for me, by the crashing about of heavy sounding objects in the trees and bushes, which were but a few yards from my post, in a scene of utter blackness which, in itself, was terrifying enough and with the nearest human contact hundreds of yards away in the darkness. I stood as far back in the sentry box as I possibly could with the fixed bayonet held firmly in front of my trembling body. The hours passed all too slowly until my relief arrived and it was perhaps as well for him and the Duty Petty Officer that their boots crunched heavily on the gravel drive giving me advance warning of their approach, otherwise they may well have been the first casualties! Later we found that the crashing in the bushes during the night watches was made by wild ponies that roamed at will throughout the forest, but I firmly believed that someone should have warned us before our first nerve-shattering night watch and its seemingly endless parade of dark terrors!

Some of the lads went to the local church on Sundays and they were mightily impressed by the sight of knightly effigies clad in the full panoply of medieval armour reclining silently in their final sleep atop their ornate tombs.

I wandered around the grounds, alone, absorbing the silent beauty of this magical place, with only the birds and flowers for company and feeling small and insignificant beneath the shadows of its lofty trees. My stay at Exbury House was a happy, relaxed time (except at night, of course) and when I returned, some fifty years later, it still exerted a magical influence on me. The tennis court net, still hung there as it had so many years ago, rotted and tattered now. There was still the uncanny feeling that the players would issue forth from the refreshment pavilion at any moment, laughing and chattering, ready to play the next set! I still regret that at no time did I enter the house itself, which was officer 'country' and out of bounds to us at all times, for I would love to have caught just a glimpse of its fabulous interior.

A single phone call and our sojourn in a country paradise was ended. Pack up and move on, but this time with a difference! I had grown to love this place, this refuge for the rich and powerful, which we plebeians had merely 'borrowed' for a short moment in time giving us an all too short glimpse into another more beautiful world and then snatching us, all too swiftly, away, back to a world of war, cruelty and stark reality! No more to shiver to the haunting, plaintive cry of the peacock, no more to wander in the silent, peaceful shadows of the mighty trees with their multi-varied tangle of wild, shaded beauty. No more to scan the weathered plaques at the base of the stripling trees in front of the stately house marvelling at the names of the 'good and the beautiful' carefully inscribed thereon. It was over, but part of my boyish heart will remain forever within that enchanted kingdom, that Paradise Lost, never to be regained!

# CHAPTER TEN

*Brighton.*

Our 'new' home was in sharp contrast to that at Exbury House. An hotel in Brighton in a street just 'round the corner' from the Grand Hotel on King Street and a much more modest establishment than its most prestigious 'neighbour' but, nevertheless, comfortable enough for us simple sailormen! My memories of our stay there are not very clear, but suffice to say it was a short one. I do remember one evening a group of us went to see Marlene Dorsey, billed as the 'Rage of Five Continents' performing a striptease at the Dome theatre and I was filled with wonder at the generous proportions of her 'upper structure'. That part of a woman's anatomy was no mystery to me, but the ones I had kissed and fondled were of the young not fully developed variety and had not prepared me for such an awesome sight. She swayed and undulated with the sensual music and had she but shrugged her creamy shoulders, I surely would have awoken next morning with two black eyes. What a woman, what a performance and what a memory to have remained so fresh after all these years.

Next day, we went to a small nearby bungalow for a typical 'pussers' medical. Although the room was large by any standards, it was 'chokka block' with young matelots and the 'medical staff', consisted of one man with a big lamp. Shuffle forward, drop the trousers and pants, quick flash on the genitals and that was it, the 'medical' was over. If, when subjected to the heat treatment, nothing jumped at the MO then all was well, you were fit! This was indeed the infamous 'crab' test which was such an important feature of Navy life and whatever else was wrong with you, physically, if you passed the crab test, you were pronounced 'fit'. The importance of this primitive 'test' was mainly because when serving aboard HM ships, each morning, hammocks were stowed in a 'netting' or cage on the messdeck and it was a fact of life that if one rating caught 'crabs' usually, the result of a 'run ashore' and a meeting with some insalubrious female within a short time, unless detected, everyone in the mess (usually about twenty men in all) had crabs too and that meant shave off and 'Blue Unction' all round, which was not only uncomfortable, but most inconvenient, if some buxom, gorgeous

89

beauty was expecting a 'frolic' during a run ashore. Not a happy position to be in for a sexy rampant matelot!

Whilst we were in various stages of undress, to my amazement, the door opened and in walked a party of young WRNS escorted, of course, by a male junior officer. They walked, seemingly not caring, across the room and vanished through a doorway at the far end closing the door behind them. Imagine, if we had walked into a room full of semi-naked WRNS what a panic would have occurred and what charges would have arisen as a result. The Navy brass didn't know how to cope with females within their ranks then and judging by recent legislation before the courts they still haven't a clue!

As there seemed to be no form of control whatsoever at the hotel, as to the coming and going of the matelots, some of them took to slipping off to London at night, leaving a phone number to call if anything untoward happened during the night, but as I suspect, the officers were doing the same thing, no-one seemed to care. After a few days we were warned to be ready to move yet again, but of course, no hint of our next destination was forthcoming. One morning the usual fleet of lorries arrived and we heaved our kitbag and hammock in the back and stood ready to move. As each name and official number was called we answered, 'Aye Sir' and stepped forward and embarked in the waiting lorry. My name was called and I duly answered the officer and stepped forward. All the official numbers called so far started with the number 3, as the ratings were fairly new entries and were Hostilities Only ratings, but I, of course, had by then served about three years and was Regular Navy and my number consequently, started with the number 1. The young RNVR Officer checking us into the lorry wasn't even wet behind the ears yet, and had no knowledge of the 'real Navy' and remarked loudly, 'You must have been a crow having that number and still an ordinary seaman?' What a buffoon, a typical know-nothing young officer, whose previous 'sailing' experience probably consisted of sailing a toy boat on the Serpentine, under the ever-watchful eye of dearest Nanny, but then of course, 'Daddy' would have been in the right 'job' to guarantee his privileged offspring officer status!

Carrying only our small brown standard issue 'pussers' attaché case, containing toilet gear and items needed for our journey to, no one knew where, we boarded the lorry and off it went. Kitbags and hammocks, had been loaded earlier and despatched so, at least, we didn't have the usual humping session to contend with!

We quickly arrived at Brighton Railway Station and disembarked from the transport. This, however, proved to be a station with a difference for it was completely empty, except for a cordon of Military and Civil Police who guarded all entrances and exits to or from the station.

Standing, huffing and puffing, at the platform was the longest train I had ever seen. The platform thronged with matelots of every shape and size but with, to me, one notable omission! There were no badges to be seen on the milling matelots' arms, which indicated that they were all new, or fairly new, entries and I began to feel a bit uneasy about the future prospects for such a large, untrained, inexperienced band of men into which I had somehow been thrust!

We boarded the waiting train with not a word being given as to our final destination and to add to the mystery, the doors were then locked and we were virtual prisoners within. I liked the situation less and less as time passed, until a whistle sounded, the train struggled briefly under the strain of its heavy load and we were off, once more, into the unknown!

We steamed steadily northwards and station names which I had never heard of were sometimes glimpsed briefly, as we slowed to pass through them and then picked up speed and rattled ever onwards.

That journey lasted twelve hours, broken only by brief stops at deserted stations, where cheerful ladies pushed laden trolleys of food and drink, usually sandwiches, cakes and hot, steaming tea along the empty platforms and served us through the windows of our 'mystery train'. Those beautiful, buxom, beaming ladies, a special wartime breed, were to appear, as if by magic, wherever I travelled during those hectic years and if any of them read this book, I want them to know that they were a source of homely comfort, warmth and spiritual uplift which extended far beyond the value of those sandwiches and welcome cups of tea which they dispensed so cheerfully and so readily! Eternal thanks, ladies! The train steamed on through the dark night and into the early dawn and we were restless now, the novelty of our journey had worn off and we wanted to be free of our confinement within the narrow 'walls' and to know what lay ahead when we attained that freedom.

The harbour at Gourock, Scotland was our mystery destination at this stage and we streamed off the train, our legs stiff and awkward, to embark on an ocean liner, named 'Empress of Scotland' formerly 'Empress of Japan', hurriedly changed when Japan stabbed America in the back at Pearl Harbour and entered the war against the Western Allies.

## USA.

The ship was administered by the RAF which, probably, was why our accommodation was in the very bowels of the ship, a converted hold space, in which we were to spend the next five days whilst at sea. It was a veritable hell-hole, from which the only escape was a long climb almost vertically up a series of ladders to the main deck and as nearly everyone was in the throes of seasickness, the long trek was too far and the unfortunate young matelots 'unloaded' their previous diet of sandwiches, cakes and tea, wherever they happened to be when they could resist no longer! Consequently, the disgusting mess hung in long festoons from top to bottom of the ladders and dripped silently on the heads of those trying to escape from the depths of the hold, and that was one time when the description of a matelot's accommodation, as the 'messdeck', truly meant what the word implied!

My unconscious mind must have been repelled by the disgusting conditions, for I fortunately, remember very little of that 'journey', but I am sure that had 'sailors' rights' been in existence then which, of course, they never were, heads would have rolled at such treatment of our 'fighting heroes' as mothers and relatives back home described them.

Suffice to say, we duly arrived in New York harbour one clear, cold night and after passing the notorious Ellis Island, where thousands of would-be immigrants, men, women and children committed suicide whilst being detained thereon and then passing the world famous 'Statue of Liberty' on Bedloe's island, a symbol of freedom throughout the endangered world, we turned and secured alongside on the waterfront.

I saw nothing of the city of New York, but I did see a mountain of bags and hammocks which had to be off-loaded, then re-loaded to be transported to 'God knows where' and I was unlucky enough to be 'detailed off' for this herculean task. The remainder of our rather wan-looking party vanished and the baggage party took over.

Eventually all was clear and loaded into yet more lorries that vanished into the night. I was too 'knackered' to care what happened next, but I remember crossing the Hudson River on a ferry, boarding a train, which to my surprise had wooden slatted seats, rather like those on the old trams in London when I was a boy, light years ago, and then arriving at Asbury Park, New Jersey and the comparative luxury of the Berkeley Hotel where we were, at last, allowed to fall into a deep, deep sleep, from which the 'Hounds of Hell' would have been hard put to wake us.

Next morning, which seemed about ten minutes after my heavy eyes closed, I awoke and believed myself still dreaming. The hotel room had been stripped of all luxury fittings but, to me, was like the palace of an Eastern potentate. There was a bath, fitted with shower at one end (a rare sight in those days for a working-class boy), towels, soap and endless hot water. The Navy must have slipped up here, was my first thought, but after a swift shower (heaven) I dressed quickly and followed the 'lads' in a quest for food which, as we descended, wasn't too difficult, given the all-pervading delicious aroma of eggs, bacon and heaven only knows what other palate-tickling gastronomic delights that filled the morning air.

A further shock awaited us when we reached the ornate Dining Hall, with its cloth-covered tables laid with 'eating tools', fresh bread, condiments, napkins and other such delights of civilised living. Behind the service counter stood American 'chefs' clad in immaculate whites, with tall, spotless hats serving breakfast on to a metal tray, with deep indentations across its gleaming surface, into which was loaded an array of mouth-watering food. My mouth was open so wide at all this incredible luxury that breakfast could have been loaded into it without touching the sides and low murmurs of appreciation and sheer happiness arose all around at the wonderful reception accorded us by our American hosts. We tucked in with great gusto and when we were asked, 'Would you like some more, there's plenty', I began to believe that it was just a dream and the stark reality of a 'Pussers' meal would be thrust upon us on awakening.

We revelled in the sheer luxury of that wonderful day and the delights that awaited us in the dining hall but, alas, the dream turned to reality and next day, as we eagerly hurried downstairs to greet our hosts, we found to our dismay, that they had slipped away, with our dream, during the night and behind the serving counter stood the reality! Pussers' cooks, complete with aprons and black galley boots!

I enjoyed a couple of 'runs ashore' in Asbury Park and when I wandered into a 'deli' and gazed, in wonder, at the serried ranks of 'pie' on offer, all hygienically displayed under covered racks, I just had to sample at least one portion of such a gastronomic delight! After long deliberation, I selected an enormous slice of blueberry pie and sitting at a nearby table, slowly and carefully consumed it, savouring fully each and every delicious morsel!

I even had a haircut, with an artistic hairdresser pandering to my every wish, but when 'pay-up time' came, the shock of forking out a third of a fortnight's pay took the shine off that occasion and I never did have a second 'trim' ashore in America.

Money, or lack of it, was of course, the biggest problem British Forces had to face in America and although the ever-generous US Government made us an allowance during our stay to help compensate for cost of living differences, we never attained the free-spending levels of US Servicemen, which was often the cause of bitter tensions between us! Time came for us to move on once more and our next destination proved to be Norfolk Navy Yard, Virginia, where we conveyed straight to the dockside, where an impressive reception committee awaited us.

There were distinguished senior Naval officers of both the American and Royal Navies, a US Navy band in full ceremonial rig, news cameras, with their large crews and a positive flood of important-looking men in smart suits talking quietly nearby!

What the hell was happening here, I thought, but that question was soon answered. We were formed into four ranks by a Royal Navy two-ringer (a rare sight of late, in this mass of Hostilities Only officers and ratings). The band struck up a festive 'air', the men in suits shuffled around a bit and the British Foreign Secretary, Anthony Eden, suddenly appeared as if by magic!

This really was a high-powered show and so unexpected by us, but apparently, the whole scene was concocted by the politicians to reveal to the world the extent of American Aid to their beleaguered British Allies and to show how the two 'Defenders of Freedom' stood shoulder to shoulder in the struggle against their common enemy!

Anthony Eden made a long speech, his opposite number replied and, of course, we cynics didn't believe a word of it, especially when A.E. assured us that we would be home before he was, a prophecy that was out by about two-and-a-half years, but what did he know anyway? The band played on manfully, the speeches, thankfully, came to an end and the important people departed, looking more relaxed now that the 'hard' bit was over and the prospect of a hearty meal seemed imminent. We were divided into small groups of about twelve men in each, seemingly without any selection process and as my group stood gazing curiously around, a handsome Sub-Lieutenant, RNVR accompanied by a tall, gangling, self-conscious, Midshipman RNVR approached and addressed us in a quiet voice. 'I am Sub-Lieutenant J.H. Howells and', turning to the 'Middy', 'this is Midshipman White. You are the crew of L.C.I. 297 and we are your officers!' We have seen a number of strange looking craft secured alongside the dock, one of them proved to be the aforementioned L.C.I. of which we had never heard before this moment in time! We had carried out training in Scotland using tank landing craft, but here we were about to live on board a craft completely different in every respect. Our long-lost kit arrived and as we ventured aboard, we found that a number of ratings were already in the messdeck, which at first glance, confirmed later, appeared to be simply a steel box containing lockers, bunks and a mess table. I quickly bagged the bunk I fancied, well away from the only ladder in or out of the mess and not against the 'ships' side. The bunks were US Navy issue and were merely a sheet of canvas lashed on to a metal frame. Until then, in the Navy, I had slept only in a hammock, so this was to be yet another new experience for me and one I quickly grew to like, which was fortunate really, for there was no alternative but the deck! Lockers were the typical pussers type and were adequate enough for my few small, personal possessions. I unlashed my hammock, spread it on the bunk, tried it for size and comfort factors and decided that at least, I would be sleeping comfortably, when the opportunity arose to do so! I looked around carefully, but little did I know that this tiny messdeck, which accommodated everyone on board, except the officers, would be my only home for the next two-and-a-half years and that I would, eventually, feel sad when the time came to leave it!

We soon settled into a daily routine, if one could call it that, for we had no coxswain, no seaman Petty Officer in charge and after the rigours and disciplines of life in the 'real' Navy, this definitely seemed a 'piece of cake' as the saying goes! Next morning at about eight o'clock, we fell in on the upper deck and the serious business of the day began. Midshipman White acted as Jimmy-the-one and called us to attention, shyly, with a deal of blushing and shuffling of feet. The 'Skipper' addressed us quietly and with confidence and I immediately noticed the contrast in style between his approach and that of R.N. Officers, who in the main, were obviously products of the 'Captain Bligh' charm school!

Our main armament consisted of four 20mm cannon, one mounted right forr'd, one aft the bridge and one either side on the deck, aft. 'Has anyone fired one of these guns before?' asked the skipper, hopefully. The crew looked suitably blank, as befits men who had never even seen such guns before! He tried again! 'Has anyone ever fired any kind of service gun before?', but to no avail and everyone looked even blanker, if that were possible, but no one answered his by now, desperate plea. 'I served in a sixteen inch gun turret', I offered encouragingly! Quick as a flash he replied, 'Right, you'll be No 1 on the forward gun' and that was my action station for the rest of my time on board and there were many times when I wished I had kept my mouth shut and volunteered no information, in accordance with the best traditions of the Senior Service! We knew nothing of such guns as previously stated, but we did possess a US Navy training manual for them and after studying the book intensively and stripping and reassembling the gun many times of our own volition, we became experts in its handling and could strip and put it back together again without any spare pieces being left over! One object on board was the subject of much derisory comment from our 'oppos' serving in tank-landing craft and it was one to which I found myself, unusually, difficult to adjust! That object was the steering gear, for instead of the traditional ship's wheel, we had a small handle, similar to those used to control tramcars back home. The helmsman sat on a high stool with a padded back rest behind a metal frame on which the 'handle' rested, with a helm indicator mounted on the forward bulkhead of the 'wheelhouse' which of course was a misnomer, for it should have been called the 'handlehouse'. The indicator read left and right instead of port and starboard and the engine-room telegraphs, front and back, instead of ahead and astern. Full speed was flank speed, and ahead and astern were forward and back! Very disturbing for a simple young sailorman, but after sailing thousands of miles across the Atlantic Ocean and around the Mediterranean then back 'home' to Scotland, steering by the dreaded 'handle', I experienced the same difficulty adjusting to the Royal Navy system, on returning to sea as quartermaster in *HMS Zest*, a fleet destroyer!

We carried a cook, a signalman, a 'sparks', a motor mechanic (Micky Mouse) an ERA, a Leading Stoker, four stokers and eight seamen, but no qualified medical staff. I was easily the youngest member of the crew at eighteen years of age and the only member not old enough to draw his 'tot', not that such a distinction made any difference aboard 297! I inherited the duty of 'medic' and with the aid of a US Navy handbook for small craft, dispensed medicines and tended the ailments of my shipmates. It is still my proud boast that, unlike many skilled doctors, I never lost a patient in two and a half years which, to be honest, was more of a tribute to the crew's fitness, than to the extent of my new-found medical 'skills'.

We carried out ship-handling runs on the river, and tugs and other local river craft quickly learned to keep well clear of those 'mad Britishers'. We secured alongside a wooden jetty at the end of which ferry boats plied their trade all day every few minutes. At first, ferry passengers stood near the edge and watched as we approached after a river trip, but after one occasion when, expecting some last minute daring manoeuvre by the mighty British Navy, we nearly demolished the jetty and sent them all sprawling, they kept a wary eye on us and withdrew to a safe distance whenever we approached.

Finding myself alone once more, not knowing anyone on board (some of the crew had trained together) I was overjoyed to see a familiar face passing by on the jetty. It was none other than that 'thumper-extraordinaire' Billy James of *Rodney* and Dagenham days and we greeted one another like long lost brothers which, in a way, we were, having joined as boys, trained together and served at sea aboard *Rodney* together! Billy was aboard an adjacent L.C.I. and we immediately arranged a run ashore together, 'just like the old days'.

Next evening, dressed in our No 1's, we proceeded to a nearby gate, guarded by an armed British matelot, this dock area being for the use of British L.C.Is exclusively and strolled, talking excitedly, some two hundred yards to the nearest bar which on entering, we found to be full of US Navy matelots, some of whom had been sniffing 'the barmaid's apron' as the saying goes. We greeted them, bought our beer and fortunately, or through long experience in Scapa Flow, Gibraltar and various other 'lively' places, turned and sat at table close to the only door. Proceedings went well. We had several beers and 'Yanks' came up telling us proudly of their ancestors who seemed to be of mainly Scottish origin. We noticed that most of the 'lads', although quite young, displayed several medals on the breast of their uniform, and Billy and I despite our, by now, three years service, had none! We asked them about the medals and were surprised to find that none had actually been to sea, but received them after training in New Mexico, the Great Lakes and other training establishments. Though sorely tempted, we made no remarks about their service in 'stone frigates', which I thought afterwards, was very civilised of us!

Billy and I were talking quietly together about the old days, when a burly figure, obviously the worst for drink, loomed before us. As soon as he spoke, I knew trouble had arrived and so did Billy, who positively thrived on it! The Yank started burbling on about the cowardly British, which I thought was a bit rich coming from someone whose country sat on the sidelines making money from our desperate struggle to survive alone, against the all-conquering German war machine and who only entered the contest when attacked by the Japanese at Pearl Harbour!

Billy and I exchanged glances and when the drunk uttered the next fateful words, I knew the moment of retribution had arrived!

'You Limies started running at Dunkirk and you ain't stopped running yet' was the last gem that he uttered, drunkenly, as Billy's mighty fist struck his jutting chin and the sheer force of the blow propelled him backward through the air, across the gangway, over the chairs and tables, to land in a crumpled heap by the wall! In almost the same movement, we two were up and away, out the door and haring along the pavement toward the dock gate and safety!

I didn't bother to glance back, but could hear the sounds of running feet and the angry yells of our pursuers. Covering the distance at a rate of knots, we could see the Navy sentry standing by the gate. He stiffened, took one look at the scene and raised his rifle as we drew closer, with the mob at our heels! Rifle to the shoulder he yelled in a loud voice, 'Halt, or I fire', as we sped past him to safety! Our pursuers, shaken by this turn of events, slowed, stopped and contented themselves with shouting obscenities from a safe distance, before losing interest and straggling away in the general direction of the bar. Fortunately for us, we knew something the mob didn't know! The sentry had a rifle but no ammunition!

I never saw Billy again after that eventful night, as shortly after we sailed for Bermuda on the first leg of our long journey to Gibraltar, but I did hear, long afterward, that he was mentioned in despatches for bravery during the crippling fire raid by the Germans on Bari harbour and later was invalided from the Service suffering from tuberculosis. Thus ended the career of a great run ashore oppo, a staunch friend and in different times, a would-be great, gutsy champion boxer!

All preparations had been made. Necessary training on these strange craft completed and we were ready to sail for Bermuda. Finally, one quiet afternoon a large van, similar to a removal truck, ground to a halt alongside and the driver ambled slowly up to the watchkeeper on duty aboard 297. 'Got some stores for you buddy', he drawled, 'Lend a hand to unload them'. The duty rating thinking it would be just a few stores walked over to help and on asking the driver which were for us, was told to his astonishment, 'All of them'.

The interior of that vehicle was a veritable Aladdin's cave of 'gastronomic goodies' to anyone from war-torn, food-rationed Britain and not one person in the crew had ever seen such a bewildering display of fruit juices, canned fruit, chocolate bars, ice cream and many other mouth-watering canned products. So great was the sheer volume of stores that the entire crew had to turn to and unload the truck. Space was at a premium and we had to fill every nook and cranny to be able to complete the task. The after troop space (rarely used) was choc-a-block with stores and we were just 'itching to get amongst them'. One seaman, who came from London, developed such a passion for pineapple, which was of the chunky variety, that he scuffed it at every opportunity and was forever known as 'Chunky' Paine and I swear, 'by my tattoo', that he eventually closely resembled a 'chunk' in physical appearance and with his closely cropped hair, looked like a 'mobile cube'.

Preparations were now complete for our departure from Norfolk Navy Yard and I viewed the near future with some trepidation. After all, we were sailing on a journey of over three thousand miles with an untrained crew, two 'green' officers, in a flat bottomed craft whose seaworthiness was still unproved. For me, personally, the transition from mighty battleship with its impregnable air to tiny, comparatively fragile, landing-craft with its 'civilian' crew was an enormous leap into the unknown and subsequent events hardly filled me with confidence! L.C.I. 297 was a Landing craft, Infantry, Large, of 150 tons displacement, 153ft long, 22ft beam, 4ft draft at the bow, 6ft at the stern, with eight General Motors 6/71 diesel engines giving 1,800hp driving twin variable pitch propellers. Their three troop spaces carried 250 troops, they had a rounded bow and a flat bottom, which did not make for comfort when under way.

Aft she carried a large kedge anchor, for pulling the craft off the beach and to help prevent her breaching to when beached. The very fact that they were of all-welded construction, an innovation in those days, was a further cause for disquiet for, after an era of welded construction, traditionalists viewed this latest shipbuilding 'fad' as dangerous and predicted that welds would split asunder when subjected to the pressures and strains of heavy seas breaking over and around them! Our 'flight' as a collection of L.C.Is was known to be fortunate in having in command a Royal Navy Lieutenant from the cruiser Nigeria, which was undergoing repairs in the USA, after being damaged while serving in the Med., and as Regular Navy officers and men were in short supply at that time, owing to naval losses and a world wide commitment, all available Regulars were employed as and where necessary and in any capacity. The great day came and fully-stored, watered and fuelled we sailed off on the great adventure into the unknown!

# CHAPTER ELEVEN

*Bermuda and beyond.*

It was now April 1943 as, with the gallant 'Nigeria' Lieutenant in the leading craft, we set off on the first leg of our long journey to Gibraltar, first port of call Bermuda!

We must have made a fine sight in our fresh paint, fourteen landing craft in line ahead and at that moment looking very professional, with our signal flags fluttering at the masthead and our rounded bows thrusting through the calm sea!

When night fell we steered a course by the white stern-light of the craft ahead and all seemed to be proceeding according to plan. Watches had been detailed off, with helmsmen organised. Cook 'wet' the tea and those off watch sat around yarning on the messdeck before turning in. We were in two watches and I had the middle and forenoon. When the watch was called, conditions had changed a bit for the worse and the motion of the craft was not so comfortable. I went forr'd to the wheelhouse and started my four hour wrestle with the ubiquitous 'tram wheel'. Sitting on the high stool, in a warm, cosy atmosphere, I began to enjoy this start to a new life with its relaxed routine, friendly 'oppo's and officers who realised that we were of the same human breed as they were!

The watch passed as many others had done in the past, with the only means of communication being the voicepipe to the bridge and the occasional course alteration or change in revs, the only sound of a human voice to be heard.

My relief duly arrived and I dived gratefully into my cosy bunk and was soon in the arms of Morpheus which, though comforting, was no substitute for the soft, warm arms of a cuddly female.

When I awoke, I seemed to be riding a bucking bronco or reliving an episode after a heavy run ashore with too much to drink and feeling the messdeck revolving around me and then I found the latter experience to be partly true. The messdeck was, indeed, revolving around me and at regular intervals there came a banging sound and a shock wave reverberating through the craft, as a powerful wave struck the flat bottom, forr'd. During the morning watch, the wind had freshened, the seas become heavier and the tiny craft was receiving a battering from both.

Staggering to the wheelhouse after a quick 'cuppa' and a fag, I observed that the helmsman looked decidedly unwell to put it mildly! For most of the young lads, this was their first taste of sea-time, apart from the Empress of Scotland 'trip' and that comparatively giant ship bore no resemblance to being at sea in this flat-bottomed 'barge'. Steering a steady course was next to impossible in this heavy sea, but using the minimum of 'wheel', I did the best I could and the 'Skipper', probably grateful at having a helmsman with some experience on board, congratulated me on my efforts, which unaccustomed praise, pleased me no end but, of course, praise unaccustomed or not always has a penalty attached to it and later, as the seamen fell by the wayside and seasickness took over, I spent more and more time at the wheel, constantly being supplied with cups of hot, steaming coffee and platefuls of delicious sandwiches by the 'chef', who seemed to be bearing up well under the strain!

Down below, some crew members were confined to their bunks, unable to eat, drink or even move in this dreadful hell into which they had been so unsuspectingly pitched and those of us who were still mobile, placed buckets and containers of any available kind beside them. That formerly clean, tidy messdeck was now a stinking hellhole, and if those supposedly little green men from outer space were to descend to earth and enter it, they would feel perfectly at home there with all those green faces around them!

Days later we crept in to harbour in Bermuda. Battered craft and weary scruffy crews, gratefully sought the sanctuary of calm, still waters and I couldn't help but think to myself what would crossing the broad Atlantic hold in store for us, after merely a few days at sea off the coast had produced such a shambles? The 'gods' must have looked down on us with favour, for all the flight survived and lived to sail another day!

The sun shone, the air was warm and the 'living corpses' soon recovered. Sounds of laughter were heard again on board as we worked hard to restore the craft to its former, pristine cleanliness and 'Chunky' Paine was seen to wander into the forepeak, clutching his 'pussers dirk', spike open, ready to pierce a can of his beloved pineapple chunks and we knew that all was well again with the world of our 'simple sailormen'. Whilst alongside, in a 'trot of L.C.Is, I 'suffered' an experience which, strangely enough, was to haunt me and to provide vivid nightmares for many years to come, long after my days in the Navy had ended and I was busily grappling with the problems of 'civvy street' and helping to bring up a family.

I was on duty one day as quartermaster on the gangway, which was, in Bermuda, about the most boring job it was possible to do. Occasionally, the QM. on the inboard craft, who was just as bored, exchanged a few words, as he too wandered around the upper deck, when suddenly I beheld a most impressive figure, clad in the uniform of Commander R.N. approaching at a fast walking pace. This was a most unexpected sight and I quickly debated with myself whether to hide or greet the great man in true Navy fashion with a smart salute. I decided to face him out and as he approached and swiftly crossed the deck of the inboard craft, I smartly sprang to attention and prepared to salute. Looking up, he failed to notice the gap between the craft and as I was about to salute, he suddenly vanished from sight and jammed in the space, up to the armpits! There was this gin-sodden, purple face, eyes popping, topped with a gold-braided cap, glaring at me from between the craft and I was momentarily stunned at the shocking sight before I sprang forward and with the aid of my 'oppo' alongside, dragged him from his dangerous position!

He grunted gruffly as Naval Officers do when confronted by a situation not 'in the book', as they say, and off he went, unsteadily on his way. I dived quickly into the wheelhouse, collapsed helplessly against the bulkhead and laughed till tears ran down my face and my head ached. Who said gangway duty was boring? It certainly wasn't that day! Months later when I had all but forgotten the incident, the memory of it returned with startling clarity!

We were in harbour and snugly turned in during the middle watch, when I and the rest of the messdeck were awakened by a sudden scream, a yell and a lot of noisy cursing. It came from 'Smolger' Smith, who was normally in the bunk above mine. Now he was standing between the bunks shouting his head off and those shouts were directed at yours truly!

'You mad bastard', he shouted in a fury, 'that's the last time I sleep above your bunk, you're bloody crazy'.

Apparently, I had had a nightmare in which I had fallen between two ships and was being crushed. Lying on my back in the bunk, I pushed with hands and feet against the bunk above occupied by

'Smolger' and such was the superhuman strength expended in my struggle to survive that I lifted 'Smolger's' bunk with him still in it, out of its socket and against the fanshaft above! Calm was eventually restored and we settled down, once more, but during that two-and-a-half years' commission, that top bunk remained unoccupied!

That nightmare was to return again and again over the years and after having been married to me for forty-five years, my wife has grown used to being pushed out of bed when it re-occurs from time to time!

The craft was soon spick and span, once more and minor repairs carried out. We were ready for the next stage in our long journey and, of course, a little more experienced this time out. We had become, overnight, a flotilla, which sounded a little more seamanlike and C.O.s met for a final conference before sailing.

I reflected, somewhat ruefully, how different my second visit to Bermuda had been from the first, which seemed light-years ago and this time, there was no luxurious lounging on golden beaches, no tea and sandwiches, no free and easy wandering around the North of the island and long, lazy days in the sunshine. Life itself is a series of peaks and valleys and the secret is to enjoy the peaks to the full and when in the valleys, look up and forward to the next peak!

Once more, stored, watered and re-fuelled, we set off across the broad Atlantic, the smallest Royal Navy craft to have done so at that time! At least we had some idea what was in store this time and we felt able to cope with most contingencies that could arise, which constituted something of an improvement in morale.

We steered at night, as before, following the sternlight of the vessel ahead and the weather was fine and clear. So far, we had no casualties from seasickness, and throughout the long journey, it was never a problem, as it had been sailing from Norfolk to Bermuda and surprisingly, such spells of bad weather experienced then did not occur!

When day broke that first morning, some craft had 'seen the light' but, unlike the three wise men, couldn't follow it, for our numbers were sorely depleted and we steamed in a wide circle, whilst the FO went looking for his missing lambs.

After a few hours, all was well again, the lambs restored to the fold and off we went across the bounding main and that was the pattern during our journey, apart for a few engine problems which proved to be, fortunately, not too serious to be solved by our inexperienced engine-room staff.

We spent our time mainly on watch or sleeping apart from routine tasks of keeping the messdeck and areas below clean and shipshape. Time passed quickly and we were soon preparing ourselves for the entry into Gibraltar and looking forward to some hectic nightlife and a few beers or so. The strange happening for me was the issuing of battledress, army boots and anklets, to be worn with the usual pussers' cap to round it off! 'Normal' working rig was bush shirt, khaki shorts and three-quarter length stockings, quite a transformation for a pusser-built lad to contend with, but I quickly realised how much more comfortable it was, both to work in and to wear ashore. I began to like this strange life in Combined Operations more and more, for it was so different in every respect from the many stupid constraints of 'pukka' Navy and one could feel a certain pride in being part of its youthful emergence into a powerful fighting force.

After seventeen days at sea, we finally reached Gibraltar and without mishap, secured alongside near the coal jetty. Our legs felt very wobbly and shaky once the motion of the craft had ceased and onshore, rolled along the jetty, like real old seadogs, which I suppose we were after completing such an epic voyage! The familiar sight of the mighty Rock, itself a symbol of British seapower, displayed proudly for all the world to see and respect; the light at Europa Point, a comforting guide after dangerous voyages through U-boat infested waters; the Barbary apes, the only wild ones in Europe, without whose presence, according to tradition, the Rock would be lost to Britain and on the West side, Alameda Gardens, then a favourite hang-out for the homosexual community, who lurked in the shadows, ready to seduce some poor, unsuspecting sailor into their ever-hungry clutches; plus, of course, the bars along Main Street packed with hard-drinking matelots ogling Spanish dancers, who gyrated to the music of colourful bands isolated high above the floor on balconies protected by wire screens, just in case some drunken matelot decided to take a pot shot at them with a bottle (empty, of course) to show his disapproval of the music, or his frustration at not being able to give one of the dancers 'one up the bracket'.

This was Gibraltar, a sailor's paradise, famous throughout the Royal Navy where 'old ships' met, drank and enjoyed the centuries-old fraternity of the sea and the subject of many a yarn around the dhobying bucket, when its joys were far away beyond reach!

Having secured, we were eager to sample the delights of shoreside, so having showered and dressed in the strange khaki and heavy boots, off we went, rolling along the jetty to the nearest bar and the bottom of the first bottle we could lay hands on.

It was customary then for the bars to display a drinks menu, chalked on a blackboard beside the front entrance and we used to start at the top and drink our way through it, usually with disastrous results, both for us and our normally immaculate clothing, but who cared? We certainly didn't and unless a major brawl started, neither did anyone else!

Next morning, carrying a monumental sized hangover, we fell in on the upper deck and were told that we would be off to Algiers in a few days, in company with the rest of our flotilla. At that precise moment we didn't care if we were off to hell, for we couldn't have felt worse than we did even there!

A few minor repairs and adjustments and we were ready for the 'off', but first came about the greatest shock of my service life so far! We were sailing that night when darkness fell but were ordered to fall in on the upper deck for a 'pep' talk by the Skipper before sailing. Accordingly, there we were, awaiting the pearls of wisdom, keyed up by thoughts of what lay ahead, when the Skipper appeared, stepping unsteadily through the wheelhouse door. Called to attention and then at ease, we were astonished when he started to speak, warning us of the perils of bomb alley, submarines and enemy warships. Be vigilant at all times, said he, his speech slurred and at times, almost unintelligible as he weaved before us. Jimmy-the-one looked suitably embarrassed and apprehensive, as well he might, for we were sailing shortly and he had a drunken Skipper to contend with.

I was utterly and completely shaken down to my deck shoes and still couldn't really take in the extraordinary situation. Naval officers acted like gods and in the power they held over the lower deck were like them, and projected an image of smooth, irreproachable efficiency and the very thought of an officer appearing drunk, even when off duty, before his crew, was completely unthinkable!

He concluded his drunken diatribe and staggered off, leaving an unhappy, shattered crew discussing this unreal situation heatedly, for we were trained to follow orders implicitly and didn't know how to cope with a drunken skipper, which even worse, left a Midshipman. RNVR in sole command!

'Let go forr'd, let go, aft,' ordered the Middy and off we went, with some trepidation, following the leader astern from the Coal jetty, bring the bows round, stop engines, then slow ahead, out into the Straits and the open sea. In the early days my entering and leaving harbour station was on the engine-room telegraphs, with the 'coxswain' on the wheel and I heard the skipper's voice down the voicepipe from the bridge, so I knew that he was still on his feet, just about.

It was then daylight and we plodded along following the craft ahead, when suddenly the engine note changed and we started to fall astern of our billet. There came a swift exchange of signals and we turned about and headed back to Gibraltar due, we discovered later, to a problem with one of the engines.

I was still on the telegraphs when we approached harbour and it was now quite dark. It was impossible to see anything of what was happening outside the wheelhouse and the coxswain and I were nervously glancing at one another with considerable trepidation when, suddenly the skipper's panic-stricken voice shouted loudly down the voicepipe, 'Astern, astern, full astern'.

I sprang into action and yanked the handles to stop, then full astern and had just completed that action, when 'crash', there was a violent collision ahead, the handle struck me between the legs and I knew no more!

When my eyes opened, the first sight was of the coxswain's chalky white face, appearing round the curtain covering the port passage entrance/exit and the craft was listing badly to port.

At that precise moment, I didn't care if I lived or died, for the pain from my battered 'wedding tackle' was intense, but I did realise that the intrepid coxswain had fled and left me to my fate! I felt sure that my blossoming sex life was ruined forever, and consequently there was now nothing to live for!

We had hit, or been hit by, an ocean-going tug, the 'Hengist' and had almost been capsized by the sheer force of the collision. At the point of impact, high on the bow, the steel had been rolled back as if by a giant hand, but fortunately there was no threat to our sea-worthiness. Frantic signals were exchanged with the station shoreside and we were ordered to anchor for the night to wait for daylight, before attempting to enter harbour. We dropped anchor, watches were set and we settled down to an uneasy night and the welcome arrival of daylight, when we crept ignominiously back into the billet we had left just a few hours ago! A court of enquiry was convened, the accident was blamed on our engine defect and the skipper lived to drink another day, of which he certainly took full advantage!

I walked about the craft for a few days like a cowboy too long in the saddle, but when the time came to put the aforesaid tackle to the test, it responded magnificently and fulfilled my wildest dreams.

After a welding job on the damaged bow, we set off once more for Algiers, to await a replacement for the faulty engine and this time the skipper appeared to be sober; and we arrived at that exotic port all in one piece and thankful to be so!

# CHAPTER THIRTEEN

*Algiers and Blondie.*

We secured alongside the waterfront, and way astern could be seen Admiral Darlan's magnificent yacht for which, of course, he would have no further use, having been rendered hors-de-cambat by an assassin's bullet. Having showered and dressed in the best 'bib and tucker', Paddy (Stoker), Mickey Mouse (Motor Mechanic) and I set off ashore to sample the exotic delights of magical Algiers and little did I know then that part of my heart would always remain buried here, with the memory of a wonderful, passionate love for an incredibly beautiful blonde from a house of 'ill repute'.

There were three brothels of note that we 'inspected' that first run ashore and, contrary to popular belief, they were not tawdry, garish dens of iniquity filled with blousy females of doubtful age and antecedents, but rather of the luxury and comfort standard of a first class hotel, with gorgeous, clean, lavishly dressed girls of seemingly all nationalities, lounging around on comfortable, spacious furniture ready and willing to chat, drink, or make love, or all three if required!

We visited the 'Black Cat', had a drink and a chat, without the rip-off for which many Soho clubs are notorious, and then moved on to the 'Sphinx' where we did the same. Moving on to the 'Half-Moon' we walked through the doorway and then I saw her! My heart raced, blood boiled and a sudden pain lanced at my heart. Trembling, I approached this vision of loveliness, who lay elegantly sprawled, limbs modestly covered on a settee in a flower bedecked alcove on the far side of the room.

She had long, blonde hair resting gently on her shoulders, with clear blue eyes, set like precious jewels in a complexion of creamy whiteness. Her luscious lips smiled welcomingly as I approached and feeling like a courtier addressing a beautiful princess, I sat down beside her and in a voice shaky with passion, I managed a soft "Hello".

She took my quivering hand and spoke with a husky, French accent, at which my beating heart tumbled over and over and threatened to burst from my youthful body! We chatted for a while and she told of her family trapped in France, who had lived in

Algiers, travelled home on a visit, and couldn't return. She sipped a drink delicately, whilst my pounding heart slowed and I thought of more practical things!

We moved upstairs to her room and sitting on the wide bed, she started to undress but I, impatient to begin, tore my clothes off in a flash and stood naked before her with 'ole Nobby' proud and erect! She opened her shapely lips and gazing up with beautiful deep blue eyes through long, silken lashes, in her most seductive voice, uttered those immortal words, 'You want fuckee fuck, or suckee suck?' and the vision was shattered!

'Both', said I, boldly and she looked up and said, 'You veree naughty boy' and who was I to disagree?

I went every day to the 'Half Moon' and spent as much time with her as was possible. I took 'Lux' toilet soap, tins of corned beef, cigarettes and anything of use to her, in those days of universal shortages and when that dreaded time arrived and her womanly cycle prevented sexual intercourse, I made love to her friend, 'Susy', a brown-skinned, Arab girl, bright and vivacious, whose sparkling laughter and fresh, open manner made her a pleasure to be with.

My 'oppos' complained as I saw less and less of them, but I was too involved in my love life to care about anyone other than my beloved! Beside loving Blondie, I truly enjoyed being in Algiers and wandering the streets, drinking in the sights, sounds and odours, which made it a fascinating city. The old fashioned 'pissoirs' were still popular in the city and whilst a screen covered the body, the legs and head were still visible as the 'gentlemen' passed water. I treasured the day when a Frenchman wearing a bowler hat was at his business, behind the screen, when a fair damsel of his acquaintance passed by. As she drew near, he gallantly raised his hat to her, presumably grasping his privy member in the other hand, to my great amusement. On another occasion, I saw a row of legs displayed and there, at the end, was a wooden leg! Try to imagine that scene taking place in London. Impossible!

Ancient trams thundered by, rocking and rattling as they did so on twin tracks and such were the numbers of 'hangers on', that they resembled a heaving mass of mobile humanity, rather than simply a means of public transport!

I wandered alone, through the Kasbah, drank thick, sweet coffee at a roadside cafe and marvelled at the numbers of ordinary Arabs, who had visited the United States and chatted away in English, with a pronounced Yankee accent, telling of their own experiences in a far-off land. I sat on a low settee and sampled the aromatic delights of the hubbly bubbly pipe and in the still, warm air, drowsily watched the world hurry by.

There were 'exhibitions' laid on in the brothels, usually at the start of business, with the obvious intention of arousing the clientele and stimulating business. I never found this at all necessary, but I did go along with the lads on occasion, and right torrid affairs they were! On a large gym mat, in the middle of the room, four, or sometimes six, naked girls performed with enormous black, rubber 'dildos', accompanied by the roars of the watching throng and another time, two naked women acted out a scenario with two Alsatian dogs, who were controlled by a little man with a whistle and every time he blew a note, the whole tableau changed round into a new position! Finally, he blew the whistle and the dogs scampered away, the girls bowed to the cheering audience and the 'show' was over!

One day, a supply ship entered harbour and secured ahead of 297, alongside the waterfront. Gangs of Arabs shuffled past our craft, carrying cardboard boxes containing bottles of beer destined for troops in forward positions. One of the lads leaned over the side and relieved a passing Arab of his heavy burden, which upset him not at all. Soon, more lads were doing the same and as the Arabs seemed quite pleased and no-one in authority appeared, this 'lifting' process went an for some time, until the lads tired of it and carefully stowing the cases in a handy troopspace, gleefully carried on with their tasks on board, anticipating the joys yet to came!

Later, they repaired to the aforesaid troopspace and set about sampling their easily acquired booty, with dire results! A huge Canadian Navy matelot who was taking passage on board somehow developed a consuming hatred of the skipper. Consequently, after consuming generous quantities of the strong beer, he decided to kill his mortal enemy and staggering along the port passage before anyone could stop him, hammered on the wardroom door, for the skipper to come out and be slaughtered. The skipper, showing great wisdom, remained where he was until 'Canada', tiring of his strenuous efforts, swayed off, to get his head down and 'sleep it off'. The skipper, meanwhile, called for assistance from the nearby Naval base and an orderly body of brawny matelots soon arrived on board, where they found, on searching the craft, several crew members in an advanced state of inebriation, whom they promptly arrested and conveyed to the Navy cell block!

I have been known, at various times in my early life, to pass on to anyone who would listen the considered opinion that women in any shape or form were trouble when taken too seriously and were simply there to be enjoyed and discarded before moving on to the next one and that 'poor old Jack' was helpless, when confronted with the wiles and animal cunning of most creatures of the female sex! On this occasion, though, my involvement with the delightful 'Blondie' had saved me from disgrace, for all the drunkenness and sinning had taken place, whilst I was locked in the soft, smooth arms, of a wily creature filled with animal cunning! The drunken lads were duly charged and sentenced to seven days' cells apiece, but as the nearest Detention Quarters at Djidjelhi were full to capacity and even had an official waiting list, the sentence was recorded but not carried out!

Our new engine duly arrived from the USA. It was quickly installed and tested and once again we were ready for the 'off', but for me, this time, I faced departure with a heavy heart, for I had to say farewell to my great love, after the happiest and most fulfilling five weeks of my young life and as that shattering moment grew nearer and nearer, I became gloomier and gloomier, until I could smile no more!

The dreaded day arrived and off I went with a heavy heart to say 'farewell'. We fell, tearfully, into each other's arms, swearing eternal devotion and I truly believed it, for the 'black dog' of loneliness, which had sat upon my shoulders for so much of my young life had, during our magical time together, faded into the background and I felt sure that such warmth and love would be beyond my reach evermore!

We sailed and, later, my messmates swore on a stack of bibles that as we made for the open sea, tears trickled down my stricken face. I naturally denied it, but man, it was a close run thing!

# CHAPTER TWELVE

*Mutiny!*

We sailed along the coast of Algeria, at one point, not too far from the spot, where, as a Boy Seaman in *Rodney*, I stood in bright sunshine, at the guardrail, starboard side, amidships, gazing idly at the veteran aircraft carrier Eagle, when she was struck on her port side by four torpedoes and quickly sank before my astonished eyes! Until then, the passage of the Malta convoy had been quiet and peaceful and we were advised by the Captain, over the tannoy, to get as much fresh air and sunshine as possible before the action started and I was still standing, staring incredulously at the spot were the mighty ship had just disappeared, when the first wave of Stukas attacked.

This time, all was quiet as we ploughed across the still, glistening sea, with never an enemy vessel or aircraft in sight. We entered Ouzou, with its mighty boom defences, remained overnight, pressed on to Bougie, then on the final leg, to Djidjelhi, where we hoped to rejoin our flotilla at long last.

There they were, tied up snugly alongside, having completed a series of night manoeuvres to prepare skippers and crews for the many hazardous operations that lay ahead. Proceeding to our billet, we managed to entangle a wire around one of the screws and next day a diver was due to arrive in order to remove it. Sure enough, early next morning, the diver arrived with his dive master, an Englishman and two Arabs, to work the air pump.

At first all went well and we leaned idly on the guardrail, lazily watching events, when suddenly, air raid red was sounded by an extremely loud siren. With a mighty bound, the two Arabs deserted the pumps, swarmed up the ladder and vanished at a rate of knots along the jetty. Bugger the diver, they must have thought, we're off! We fell about laughing, until the anguished voice of the dive master called for help with the pumps. Paddy and I jumped on to the jetty, swarmed down the ladder and started pumping, still laughing, for the D.M. filled the air with so many choice oaths and foul words about Arabs in general and the two deserters in particular, that I laughed until tears ran down my cheeks and my head ached!

Next day we received a signal that 297 would proceed to sea that night on manoeuvres in order to catch up on the exercises missed due to our late arrival at the base. I had a premonition that all was not to go well with this night mission and in the light of subsequent events, I must have gazed into a crystal ball unknowingly, and seen future 'happenings' portrayed therein, for it was a disaster even before it started!

The skipper was as pissed as a fiddler's bitch, and as I unknowingly was preparing to let go, a seamen rushed up to me and said, breathlessly, 'Have you seen the skipper, Sam, he's as pissed as a pudding and he's on his way to the bridge?'

I had heard matelots' yarns before, so decided to see at first hand what was happening and sure enough there he was, swaying and stumbling about and muttering to himself!

That was enough for me and I moved swiftly to the wheelhouse where some other crew members had gathered.

'What shall we do?' one of the stokers cried.

'You can all do as you like,' I replied, 'but I am not going anywhere with the skipper in that state. I'm too young to die and besides, I'm much too handsome.'

Someone giggled nervously and as more crew members arrived, chattering away, they said, 'We're with you, Sam,' to which I replied, forcefully, 'No you're not, I'm on my own and so are you!'

Jimmy-the-one arrived on the scene and putting on a stern air, unlike his usual self, ordered everyone to their stations for leaving harbour. No one moved and he repeated the order even more sternly. There was a shuffling of feet and I thought, momentarily, that the crew would break away but they stood firm.

He reappeared with the skipper in tow, and he was carrying a clip-board, with a blank sheet of paper attached. I was on the end of the line and he approached, swaying gently in the evening breeze and reeking of drink. 'I order you to carry out your duties,' he mumbled, with several stops and starts, 'and what do you say to that?'

Taking care to keep a reasonable distance between us, just in case he fell on top of me, I replied firmly, 'I am not going to sea with you in that condition, sir.'

He tried to write my reply on the blank sheet, but with no success and before he could move on to the next in line, an officer's plummy voice cried, 'What's the hold-up, old boy, I can't move until you do?'

Receiving no reply, he athletically leaped the guardrail and took in the situation with a quick glance. He took the skipper by the arm and led him away, presumably to the wardroom, for we saw him no more that night! The officer returned and saying nothing, vaulted the guardrail and was gone.

He must have contacted the barracks, for shortly afterwards, a stern looking RN Bosun came on board and after a few words with the Jimmy, came towards us, at which most of the lads vanished through the open wheelhouse door, leaving Mick and I alone to face him!

He spoke to me kindly and said that he was aware of the situation and would be taking the craft outside the harbour with the other vessels, but that we would anchor outside and re-enter with them in the morning! 'O.K., lad,' he said and I replied, 'Aye, Aye, Sir,' in my most seamanlike fashion, at which he smiled and turned away.

I doubled smartly to my station and stood by to leave harbour as did the remainder of the crew and shortly, off we sailed and did exactly as he had promised.

Next day, we entered harbour, in line ahead with the rest of the flotilla secured alongside and the bosun departed, after seeking me out and saying, 'Well done, lad,' to my intense and grateful surprise. The skipper was on his feet, life returned to normal and no more was heard of the incident!

I never went ashore in Djidjelhi, but some of the lads did and despite the cell sentence overhanging them, raided the NAAFI stores by forming a human pyramid and forcing an upstairs window, from which they dropped cases of beer to those waiting below. I saw no available women there so stayed on board and looked to the future.

Shortly, the whole flotilla left Djidjelhi, en-route for Sousse, in Tunisia, visiting Philippville, where the old cruiser, Vindictive, was now a base repair ship, then Bone, Bizerte, Tunis, finally arriving in Sousse, situated on the Gulf of Hammamet, where we were to be based before embarking troops for the Invasion of Sicily.

Those serving in Landing craft, Combined Operations, were in a difficult position where the other conventional services were concerned. There had arisen a sea of jealousy over the appointment of Lord Louis Mountbatten as Chief of Combined Operations over the heads of many senior officers who considered that his Royal connections had favoured his promotion before that of more qualified officers, who had no powerful sponsors to push their case, thereby advancing their prospects. We landing-craft personnel belonged to no one and therefore no one Service would assume responsibility for us in matters of stores and supplies of any kind which, at times, lead to difficulties in obtaining food and clothing and I can state with full honesty that the Americans were far more generous to us than any of our own Services, who just didn't want to know us. We were, therefore, primarily scavengers and anything not firmly 'nailed down' we considered ours for the taking. So much so that one day, all landing-craft personnel were ordered by the Senior Naval Officer, Sousse, to muster on the parade ground, in the barracks, where he delivered a blistering attack on us concluding with these words: 'You are nothing but a gang of pirates and anyone appearing before me will be for the high jump, I assure you.'

I would like to have dragged that snooty bastard, with his stiff collar and cuffs, from the soft comfort of his quarters, with good food and wine at his command, on board any of the L.C.Is and force him to experience the primitive conditions that we endured without complaint! Shortly, however, masses of American Army troops arrived at the port and commenced embarking in L.C.Is bringing with them the usual massive amount of stores and 'goodies' of all descriptions. Thanks entirely to our American allies, our food supply problems were over for the time being and the well-deck forr'd was stacked with a bewildering assortment of cases of mash, K-rations, tins of fruit and many other items, which to us, were sheer luxury and to the Americans, just normal rations, about which they were always griping!

The soldiers of the American 1st Infantry Division were a cheerful, happy crowd and we always enjoyed having them on board, after this first experience of their jocular, bantering style.

Night fell, and we put to sea part of a mighty armada of ships of all sizes, shapes and capabilities, many of which we had never seen before. This was obviously the much talked of 'Big One' and in spite of the boisterous atmosphere on board, we anticipated our first 'big' landing with mixed feelings of fear and excitement.

During the night, the weather deteriorated and we blundered along in rough seas and black darkness, with an occasional glimpse of ghostly shapes all around us, in the darkness of the night.

Once, with a loud, nerve-shattering roar, an enemy aircraft dived swiftly out of the gloom and dropped a single bomb, which thankfully, fell harmlessly in our wake, but that proved to be the only sign of an enemy presence, during our approach to the island of Sicily and the initial landings.

Landing ramps forr'd were winched out, ready for the troops quick move ashore and the men fiddled with and adjusted their kit and weapons, ready for the 'off'. I and my guns crew consisting of Paddy (Stoker) and Geordie (Chef) were closed up on the forr'd Oerlikon, gun cocked and ready to fire, if needed, with spare drums of ammunition by the ready-use locker.

From our position high on the bow, we looked down below at the landing ramps and at the moment we hit the beach, the guns crew were the nearest point to the enemy and we had an assortment of weapons handy, just in case they fancied a trip around the harbour at our expense.

It was quiet as we beached, and the troops disembarked waist deep in the chilly water and waded ashore.

Suddenly all hell broke loose and shells started to fall around us, as we winched off the beach and headed out to the nearest troopship carrying reinforcements, where we loaded up and headed back to the beach. This was the pattern of the next thirty-six hours. Load up, beach. Load up, beach, until we seemed to be moving as in a dream and the whole scene became unreal. Once, as we headed for the beach and just as we were passing an American trooper, fully loaded, an aircraft swooped from the sky, dropped one small bomb and sped off. The bomb struck the trooper a glancing blow on the bow and exploded. To our amazement, bodies started to fly through the air as the men abandoned ship, even those well away from the area of the small fire that broke out, including amidships and right aft. That really was hitting the beach the hard way and I expect that many of them drowned in the process.

The 1$^{st}$ Infantry Division ran into some unexpected heavy opposition, after their successful landing at Gela (Dime) on 10$^{th}$ July, 1943 and at one point, German tanks were within two thousand yards of the beach, firing on American supply dumps and on landing craft. 297 was ordered to return to the beach and stand by to re-embark men of the 1$^{st}$ Division. General Conrath, at one point, signalled that pressure from the Hermann Goring Division had forced the enemy to re-embark his forces, but a combination of field artillery and naval gunfire forced the Germans to retire with heavy losses, and we left the beaches and lay offshore.

That night, General Patten's attempt to reinforce the Gela front by air proved to be disastrous, for having received no advanced warning of large numbers of aircraft flying overhead, when the aircraft carrying 504 Combat Team flew over the assembled armada of warships, every ship opened fire (including 297) and inflicted horrific casualties on the unfortunate paratroopers.

Next morning we were ordered back to the beaches to embark Italian prisoners of war and transport them to Tunis for internment. We approached the beach and an amazing sight greeted our astonished eyes, for it was a teeming mass of scruffy, lice-ridden Italian soldiers, who looked more like a collection of thieves and beggars than a military force, supposed to be defending their homeland. I was shocked at their filthy condition and unmilitary bearing, but the sudden appearance of two German aircraft quickly switched my mind to other things, but strangely enough, they ignored our presence and attacked the seething mass of their so-called allies, who understandably, scattered, screaming and shouting in all directions. My sympathies lay with the Germans, for with such pathetic allies, whose disastrous performance in the Western Desert, Abyssinia, Greece and in Sicily itself, must have caused the loss of many a proud German soldier. I felt that shooting was much too good for them and that they were a disgrace to the military profession!

When things cooled down a bit, we embarked about 300 Italian prisoners and sailed for Tunis and I suppose that we were fortunate that our passengers were not at all warlike, for at sea, at any given time a mere six or eight of us, at most, were on watch, whilst the remainder, were sleeping or working below and would have been overcome by sheer weight of numbers, if they had decided to take over the craft. A couple of days at sea and the crew became restless and took to scratching and wriggling, when thinking themselves unobserved and as an 'old sailor', I soon realised what had happened! We had all got 'crabs', in fact, they were so numerous that the crabs had us! I challenged some of the lads to a show of groins and sure enough, there they were, the dreaded mobile blackheads, as they were known!

Out came the US Navy medical book for small craft and turning its pages, I soon found a solution to our problem. Raw vinegar, no less and we quickly raided the stores, where fortunately, a generous supply proved to be available, so it was down trousers and splash it on, all over, an expression that became very famous years later.

I duly stepped smartly up to the bridge to inform the skipper, who, as I approached, was wriggling and scratching in a most ungentlemanly fashion. His jaw dropped when I informed him of the unwelcome stranger in our midst and he muttered despairingly, 'What can we do, Garrod?'

'Never fear,' cried I (the most junior rating on board) 'Get the vinegar out.'

He gazed at me, suspiciously, but then his officer training came to the fore and he must have thought, 'He wouldn't dare!'

'Thank you, Garrod,' said he and added, gratefully, 'You're doing a good job.'

'Thank you sir,' I replied, moving away quickly in case his crabs were lonely and decided to merge with mine.

'Twas only a little thing that I did that day, but from then on, the skipper seemed to regard me in a different light and later, when I suffered a series of punishment duties, mainly through slipping ashore in my insatiable search for 'crumpet', he treated my indiscretions both with fairness and leniency!

L.C.I. 297 smelt like a mobile fish and chip shop, at least our part did, but the formally pristine, troop spaces smelt like the underside of a scrofulous tramp's armpit and on arriving in Tunis, we soon found out why! In every space there was a small toilet with a foot pump to remove the effluent into the sea, outside, but such refinements were, unfortunately, beyond the comprehension of the simple Italians, who started crapping into the pan and when it was full, stood on the seat and crapped some more, until each one contained a quivering, stinking mass, well above the seat level!

I was stripping down a gun, which was our normal routine after being at sea, when the coxswain hove alongside and muttered, a bit sheepishly, I thought, 'leave that Sam, it's all hands to cleaning stations'.

'When I've finished this job,' I replied, pleasantly enough!

'Now,' he said, forcefully'.

'Piss off,' I replied, equally forcefully and he did.

I carried on working, still in quite a relaxed mood when the 'Jimmy' ambled up. 'I understand you have refused to carry out an order,' said he blushing!

'Yes, sir,' I replied, and with great patience explained my reasons for doing so! Off he went and I carried on working once more, when suddenly, he was back.

'The Captain wants to see you, in the wheelhouse,' he said and, on hearing the unusual 'Captain' bit, I knew it was serious so, downing tools, off I went in Jimmy's wake.

We went through the routine once again and I dared to ask what was so important a task that it could interfere with established procedure, to which the skipper replied, 'You are here to carry out orders, not to query them,'' but he did tell me what the job was. Yes, it was all hands to cleaning out the toilets, which of course, should have been done by the stinking Italians before they left the craft.

My patience snapped and I said, 'If I wanted to be a shithouse cleaner, I would have stayed in civvy street, sir!'

'Fourteen days stoppage of leave,' he ordered sternly and I was dismissed! Passing along the upper deck, I came upon a miserable gang, clad in overalls and incredibly, wearing gas masks carrying buckets of foul, wobbling, stinking crap to be dumped onshore and I laughed so much as they slunk off that I nearly missed the top step and fell down the ladder!

Later, teams of American Army disinfestation squads arrived on board with their enormous flit guns, from which they sprayed DDT powder everywhere, including in our lockers and bedding and they even gave us a couple of tins each, in case the crabs returned for another go!

In the evening, after tea, I was issued with a wire brush and spent two hours brushing the wire towing pennant, which was stowed around the superstructure base, but the lads forgave my laughter and rallied round their 'suffering' comrade and plied me with bottles of booze, cigarettes, cups of tea and anything else that was going and my evening task became quite a social occasion on board, and anyway, we were off to sea before my punishment was completed!

I had many more spells of punishment and we were fortunate that the towing pennant was never used, for had it been, my constant wire scrubbing had so diminished its circumference, that at the slightest tension, it would definitely have parted!

# CHAPTER THIRTEEN

*Sudden death.*

Being in all respects ready for sea, we duly sailed, bound for the port of Syracuse on the east coast of Sicily, where there was a large, artificial harbour, which included a seaplane base at the northern end. After an uneventful journey, we arrived at the port and dropped anchor, well offshore, practically in the centre of the bay.

There were sporadic attacks by single German aircraft, usually from North to South of the anchorage, which were more of a nuisance value than anything else, but one day we received a terrible shock.

This time the aircraft approached from the east, the narrowest point of the harbour. Beached onshore, unloading thousands of gallons of fuel was an American LST. The lone aircraft headed straight for it and dropped a single bomb scoring a direct hit!

There was a terrific explosion and within seconds, where there had been a busy scene of an approximately 1500 ton Landing Ship, surrounded by working parties unloading its precious cargo, there remained a heap of twisted metal amid a terrible picture of utter carnage, with dead and dying men scattered around it! We stood unbelieving and shocked beyond comprehension at the sheer suddenness of the tragedy, hearing the screams of so many badly wounded men who, a few moments before, laughed and joked as they worked in the warm sunshine.

We were short of food again, and to the north of us, at anchor, lay an American Liberty ship, so three of us, Mick, Paddy and myself, decided to pay them a visit and, if possible, scrounge some grub from them! Accordingly, we unshipped the rubber dinghy from its stowage and paddled off toward our American allies.

We three were clad only in khaki shorts and 'sandals' improvised on board from pieces of wood with strips of canvas secured to the sides and, with afterthought, we must have looked very much like a gang of pirates, as described by the snooty Naval officer in Sousse, but we didn't think of it at the time, foremost in our minds, was the quest for 'grub'.

The usually hospitable Yanks couldn't believe, at first, that this scruffy bunch was part of the mighty Royal Navy, but when they heard my cockney accent and we denied, proudly, having any connections with the R.N. and were, indeed, Combined Operations personnel and had landed the American 1$^{st}$ Infantry Division safely at Gela, their generosity knew no bounds.

They 'lashed' us up to ice cream, hot dogs, cans of coke (their ships were dry) and sent us on our way, rejoicing, with a full sack of freshly-baked bread which, after subsisting on pussers 'hard tack' for weeks on end, was heaven indeed!

Our happy state was short-lived, however, for on paddling towards 297, we observed the skipper's angry face peering over the guardrails. During our absence, he had received sailing orders, but on calling the hands to prepare for sea, he found, to his disgust, that three of his crew were missing and as in 'Little Bo Peep', no one knew where to find them! Another fourteen days stoppage of leave, but as we shortly sailed, that was a futile punishment, anyway!

This time we headed up the coast to Messina to prepare for the landings on the 'Toe of Italy' at Reggio, Calabria.

When that took place, it was a piece of cake, as they say, and our only danger came from the shells fired by our own guns, whilst the landing was unopposed, at which we complained not at all.

Charlie Chester and his wife arrived in Messina to entertain the troops, along with several other entertainers, but we drew the short straw and conveyed the Western Brothers across the Straits, who, after coming aboard, took to the wardroom and were seen no more by us until they disembarked in Reggio!

Meanwhile, Charlie Chester and Beryl (I think) crossed in a tank landing craft and on the way, Charlie played the piano in the hold and his friendly wife baked bread for the lads in the tiny galley. A good time was had by all on board the TLC.

We returned to Messina and beached away from the town, at a quiet spot, with the ramps still inboard. Rapidly, a crowd, mostly women, waded through the clear, warm sea, the water coming up to their waists. We gathered forr'd and knowing that the people were very short of food, whilst, as was usual after a landing, our well-deck was fairly filled with Army rations left behind when the troops landed, we started dropping tins of mash, hash and various types of food down to the waiting assembly.

The women were giggling and laughing and really enjoying the situation, which was of course, harmless enough, as we couldn't get near to them when, suddenly, a brawny, swarthy-looking man waded towards us shouting at the top of his voice and gesticulating wildly! One woman, of striking appearance, with her long, black hair streaming wildly around her beautiful face and who was heavily pregnant, had just caught in her apron one of the tins, when the man arrived on the scene. He screamed at her and dealt her a mighty whack in the face knocking her backwards into the water. He then grabbed hold of her hair and dragged her through the sea back to the beach, yelling as he did so and intermittently, whacking her face with his clenched fist.

We were horrified, but could do nothing to help the unfortunate woman and the rest of the crowd simply carried on, without turning a hair! We called him all the bastards under the sun and many other choice words as well, but he took no notice of our shouts and on reaching the beach, vanished from view, still kicking and punching the woman as he did so!

Italy had surrendered and the Germans started a mass evacuation of Allied prisoners of war held in camps in northern Italy within a few hours of the Italian defection. There were some 75,000 British prisoners held in these camps, but around 10,000 managed to escape, many helped by the local civilian population. Information was filtered through to them that various rendezvous points had been set up, along the coast and anyone reaching them undetected by the Germans, would be rescued by landing craft specifically despatched for that purpose.

This was 297's latest task and we sailed along the coast, out of sight of land and when darkness fell, crept silently inshore and with engines stopped, all lights extinguished and a strict no talking or smoking rule, lay there till just before dawn, when we sneaked out to sea again, where we lay waiting for the next night!

This was a nerve-wracking business and one night, in particular, we lay inshore, everyone at action stations, in case of detection, when a train loaded with German troops passed by on the coastal railway, with lights blazing, so that we could clearly see them at the windows. What a beautiful target, right in our sights and so close, but it was not to be!

Opening fire would undoubtedly have caused many casualties from our three Oerlikons at that range, but would also have compromised our mission and could have lead to the capture of the very men we were there to assist. I would very much like to be able to say that our efforts were successful, but after four or five nights, no-one had arrived at the rescue points and we were all very disappointed at the lack of results!

The great battle at Salerno was being bitterly fought at this time, but we were many miles away and saw nothing of it.

Our next spell in action was at Termoli, where we sneaked inshore, once again, with a Special Raiding Force composed of SAS, Long Range Desert Group and Commandos who, undetected, managed to reach the main cross-roads through the town and lay silently, while German reinforcements in lorries passed by their covert positions, which they had to hold, until the main force arrived.

We slipped out to sea again and returned later, accompanied by three other L.C.Is with the vital reinforcements, who achieved complete surprise and by 1800 that day, the town was taken after fierce fighting around the railway station.

We were attacked once by a single German fighter, with machine-guns blazing, while still in the harbour, but it happened so quickly that the action was over in seconds, without casualties on our side. We left harbour and anchored a few hundred yards offshore, and there I experienced the biggest fright of my life so far!

We were not closed up at the guns then and I was caught in the open, on the upper deck aft, when several German aircraft dive-bombed our little group of L.C.Is. Normally I would have been at the gun and in the heat of action, concentrating too much on firing it, to bother about how dangerous it was, but this time I was alone with no cover and no weapon and I didn't like it one little bit! I ran for my own gun, right forr'd, when there were two guns, ready to fire, close by, aft, and as the aircraft turned and swooped down, machine guns blazing, I dived, head first, through the nearest door as they sped away!

After Termoli, where from outside the harbour we watched a tank battle raging, as German forces attempted to hold up the Allied advance without success. We carried on our 'leapfrog' operations behind enemy lines and as the Germans fell back to previously prepared defence lines, we simply landed troops to their rear, or carried out raids on their supply lines, forcing them to fall back once more!

Sea power was the key to the whole plan and had the Italian Navy been the formidable force it purported to be pre-war, then the whole Italian campaign would have been a totally different story!

Control of the seas enabled the Allies to land practically at will and, after putting the Armies ashore, landing craft were able to supply them with reinforcements, ammunition and supplies with impunity!

We carried on behind enemy lines at Brindisi, Bari and Barletta and at the former, with a feeling of great joy, I had the pleasure of making the acquaintance of the superb Italian women, and having been disgusted at the performance of their menfolk on all counts, found them to be, indeed, something else!

Long, black hair tied loosely behind the head; dark, flashing eyes, curvaceous bosom and hips; skin like a she-mouse's fore and after, and a fiery temperament made them completely irresistible to a simple old sailorman such as I and, compared to their volcanic charms, all other women appeared pale, lifeless and unattractive.

'Nobby' awoke from a deep slumber and started putting himself about a bit, with great alacrity, anxious to fulfil his vital part in cementing Anglo-Italian relations and endeavouring, to the best of his ability, to make up for time wasted in war-time pursuits.

I was eighteen years of age, five feet nine inches tall, weighing approximately ten stones five pounds, with fair, curly hair, blue eyes and a richly tanned, slim body, which the women apparently loved, so crumpet was no problem at all, though of course, the tins of corned beef, bars of soap and other small 'luxuries' were a great help!

In Barletta, I 'took up' with a dark eyed damsel in a 'chestnut shop' and as she spoke some English, things went really well! At the back of the shop, behind a striped curtain, was a small room with a single bed and that was our own private 'love nest', where we spent many happy, loving hours and if a customer entered the shop, which was not often in the afternoon, that being siesta time, she would cry 'Uno momento' in an anguished voice and they departed, leaving us to our pleasures.

What a delightful, understanding people they were, with a strong sense of the priorities of life!

*Yugoslavia.*

We started carrying out nocturnal runs to Yugoslavia, ferrying medical supplies and ammunition to the partisans, but their sense of gratitude was, unfortunately, not visible, for they seemed to resent our very presence, although we undertook great risks to assist them! To make the journey, it was necessary to pass through a restricted zone during darkness, which was patrolled by British destroyers who, believing themselves to be the only Allied shipping in the area at that time, were not averse to opening fire at anything that moved, without wasting time by asking too many questions.

L.C.I.(L) 108 was spotted at night by a patrolling destroyer who promptly put a four-inch shell through her forr'd troopspace which, although she did not sink, put an end to her operations in that area! Some time later, on a visit to Malta for repairs, we saw her empty hulk swinging round a buoy in Grand Harbour.

On a later occasion, carrying a military mission dedicated to assisting the partisans in their fight against the Germans, who had ravaged their country, we crept along the deeply wooded coastline where nothing was visible except an old jetty, which we secured alongside to await the arrival of the partisan group. When they did appear, they looked a villainous, suspicious lot, for all the world as though we had come to kill them rather than to help and, at first, they refused to allow the mission to set foot on the jetty. After much haggling and argument, they grudgingly allowed our party to land and led them, in stops and starts, along the jetty, to vanish into the dense woods. We stood, watchfully, at the guns, prepared for any act of treachery by them, but all was quiet, as we prepared to leave!

We were mightily impressed by the women, who looked even more sinister than their male colleagues and were, indeed, much bigger. They were festooned with bands of cartridges, with grenades dangling around their waistlines (just visible) and made me very nervous, as they stared in an unfriendly, moronic fashion at us. If we moved, their baleful eyes followed every inch of movement and I gained the impression that they would have loved to set about us and, after hearing from our own soldiers how they had treated their own countrymen, who happened to support a different political persuasion from theirs, I wouldn't have hesitated to return their fire one instant!

Not only were they conducting a war, of sorts, against the common enemy, but they were busy killing their own people at the same time with weapons supplied by the Allies!

I knew that 'Nobby' definitely didn't fancy them, for he had shrunk so much from their very gaze, that only the rim of his 'bobby's helmet' prevented him falling back inside!

Dubrovnik was very beautiful to behold, but the people there were sullen and unfriendly. The joys of Communism had obviously, escaped them so far!

# CHAPTER FOURTEEN

*Suffer little children.*
We sailed for Pozzuoli some three kilometres west of Naples, with a small port which was filled to overflowing with L.C.Is, mostly American, with their distinctive taller bridge structure and immaculate overall finish, which was a far cry from our wire-brushed, red-leaded, pussers' 'crabfat' rough exterior.

Life settled quite pleasantly into a relaxed, cosy routine, but of course, we were well aware that something 'big' was afoot. There was shore leave and we were soon fixed up with a beautiful 'partner' ashore. 'Demon Vino' was of a better quality than that in Naples and we soon established a regular source of supply, which was less likely to send us blind, as had happened elsewhere.

Frequently, a fat, well-fed priest would waddle aboard and presenting a pasteboard card, would solicit money or goods 'for the children'. It didn't take long for us to realise that the priests were fat and the large numbers of young children who lived on the streets were extremely thin, so where did the 'goodies' go? Obviously not to the children, so we devised a scheme to redress the balance and benefit the ragged, ill-fed waifs who daily begged for food and cigarettes, which were the most popular form of local currency.

We still had cases of American tinned food in the well-deck, so, in the forenoon, we opened the cans in the galley, tipped the contents into a large cooking pot and slowly heated the resulting mass, until it was ready for dishing out to the kids.

In the forr'd troopspace we erected long tables and wooden benches and plates for a dozen 'diners'. We then went to the gangway and ushered on board twelve of the urchins hanging around there. Escorting them to the troopspace, we invited them to sit and 'scoff' the hot food as we carefully placed it before them.

Their dirty faces were a wonder to behold. At first suspicious, as all street children have to be in order to survive, then they beamed and without further ado, got stuck in and demolished the food piled on the plate before them, in double quick time. Watching their sheer enjoyment, I wondered when and if, they had enjoyed such a meal before? At that precise moment, I would loved to have fed the starving children of the world, just for the pleasure of seeing the happiness shining on their pinched, neglected faces!

When they had finished eating, there came the 'serious' bit, when they had to 'earn' their meal by singing for us a little song, the words of which went something like this:

BISCUIT FOR BAMBINO, NIENTO MUNGERIE,
CIGATETTI PAPA, CHOCOLATI ME!

They sang their hearts out and then, as we escorted them back to the gangway, we gave each child five cigarettes and off they went laughing and singing their 'new song', leaving us all in a state of some emotion. We had our 'sing song' every day, while in harbour and the fat priests gave up and bothered us no more!


We sailed next to a small Yugoslavian port, whose name I know not, taking the usual supplies and ammunition, and this time, the crazy behaviour of those we had come to help could, without Service discipline, have caused a major tragedy.

We secured alongside the jetty, the only vessel of any description to be seen there and were duly unloaded, by both men and the intimidating 'women' partisans, of whom we kept well clear at all times. We cleaned ship, then settled down to the usual routine of dhobying, writing letters, flaking out on the bunk, reading or simply spinning a yarn, as sailors love to do, as you may be aware from reading this book! Suddenly, the 'Jimmy' appeared at the top of the messdeck ladder. 'All hands fall in on the upper deck'', he called dramatically and vanished, forr'd. We tumbled up the ladder swiftly, impressed by his unusual manner and falling in on the upper deck, were surprised by the appearance of the skipper who, looking serious, informed us that an Allied aircraft had come down in the sea in our vicinity and 297 was detailed to search for it and its crew.

We needed no urging and within minutes, the craft was slipping from alongside and heading for the open sea at full speed. On nearing the search area, every available man was posted on lookout duty, even offwatch stokers, the 'chef' and anyone else who could be roped in. We searched for hours, eyes straining anxiously, praying that an oil slick, an item of clothing, or any clue to the whereabouts of our unfortunate comrades might be spotted, but to no avail!

Darkness was falling and reluctantly, the skipper decided to abandon the search and return to harbour. The crew remained on lookout, long after we had left the area, hoping against hope to see something of the missing men, but it was not to be and we approached harbour with heavy hearts, without the usual banter and leg-pulling that characterised a return to a comparatively safe haven.

We were at stations for entering harbour and I was right forr'd, high on the bow, close to my faithful Oerlikon when, as we turned to starboard towards the jetty, all hell broke loose. A fusillade of small arms fire rang out, directed at us and I heard a groan from amidships and saw 'Smolger' go down, clutching his leg.

With a hail of bullets whistling past my head, I let go the headrope and dived over the gunshield, which was about four feet high, swung the gun towards the jetty and was about to return fire, when the skipper screamed desperately, 'No firing, no firing'.

I would love to have given those mad bastards a dose of their own medicine and they definitely wouldn't have come back for more!

We finally secured alongside the jetty and the skipper went ashore to remonstrate with the local partisan leader. Personally, I would have shot the bastard, whatever the consequences for Anglo-Yugoslav relations which, from landing-craft crews point of view, were at an all-time low anyway!

We all felt better when we prised 'Smolger's' tightly gripping hands apart, expecting to see an open wound and saw only a deep dent in the skin, where a spent bullet had struck and I assure you, we did not allow him to forget the fuss he made on receiving his 'war wound'.

Shortly afterwards, we sallied along the coast once more, at dead of night and took on board a dozen or so of partisan wounded, which included a young boy, about nine or ten years of age, who had been carrying messages at night to his local partisan group, when he was challenged by a German patrol who, when he took cover and failed to reply to their challenge, opened fire in the darkness and hit him in the leg just below the knee. In spite of the intense pain of his wound, he did not cry out and was rescued by his comrades, who managed to persuade a local doctor, who would have been himself shot if discovered, to operate on the leg and remove it below the knee. When we saw him, in the light of day, he was quite chirpy and hobbled about the craft on a crutch made from the branch of a small tree, with the cross piece under his arm covered with strips of what looked like old rags.

For those who claim that men have no sensitive feelings, I wish they could have seen the way in which those rough, uneducated men cared for that small, wounded boy, who was never left on his own, was waited on hand and foot and helped to smile and overcome his disabilities!

We were overjoyed to be informed that this time, our destination was Malta and we would accompany the partisan wounded to a rest camp, set up in what used to be the Royal Marines Camp to the north of the island.

The seas were calm and smooth and we glided along, sometimes in bright moonlight and by day, in warm, comforting sunshine, in what could be described on board as a holiday atmosphere.

At night, in the moonlit well-deck, forr'd, our Yugoslav passengers sang traditional folk and national songs in a surprisingly harmonious style, which conveyed at times deep sadness and longing for faraway homes and loved ones and alternately, joy and happiness in perfect contrast.

My feelings towards partisans in general mellowed a little, well, towards this group anyway and I understood the turmoil and suffering they had been forced to endure in order to satisfy Hitler's mad dreams of world domination!

In the camp, we did exactly as we pleased and when we pleased and if we wanted to sleep in, we did so and turned out when we were good and ready. The food was excellent and plentiful and we were waited on hand and foot for five glorious, unforgettable days!

The Yugoslavs did as they pleased also and they carried the boy on their sturdy shoulders about the camp and into the warm, clear sea and the sound of his happy laughter was a sheer tonic to our war-jaded ears and hearts.

Our stay ended all too soon and we returned on board and to reality, refreshed and ready to face whatever new challenge lay ahead.


*Naples.*

We put to sea once again, destination Naples, and arrived safely after an uneventful voyage. We secured alongside in Naples itself and the harbour was a mess of sunken ships, surrounded by heaps of rubble, which had probably once been fine buildings. There was no shore leave, as there was a raging epidemic of typhus in Naples, and there was also great incidence of VD, which the Italians seemed to regard as being in the same category, medically speaking, as the common cold! I had heard the expression, 'dressed like a pox-doctor's clerk' but I thought it was just an expression and nothing more until Naples, where pox-doctors abounded and their 'clinics' were everywhere!

Mick and I decided to chance our luck ashore and accordingly, when darkness fell, we sneaked ashore and dodging the jeep patrols of Military Police were soon safely ensconced in the comforting arms of Bacchus and his close ally, Aphrodite, and oblivious to the cares and perils of the world outside!

Night after glorious night, Mick and I swam in a sea of ecstasy in the soft, tender arms of our new-found loves, but, alas, the Sword of Damocles fell with sudden swiftness upon our bemused heads and after a night of glorious passion, we crept back through the heaped rubble, just as the stern line was being cast off and out we stepped, in full view of the Skipper and the Jimmy who, at least, to give them some credit, had the grace to look relieved at our apparent reincarnation!

Under punishment again, a state which was fast becoming the norm, but, of course, had the craft sailed without us, we would have been in even worse trouble, so we had something to be grateful for.


*Hopping time!*

There next occurred an episode, in which all my years of Naval training went by the board and I fell from grace, succumbing to the evils of demon drink!

I was under punishment, as usual, but I had by now wire-brushed the towing pennant so many times, that it was difficult to find it, let alone brush it, so I was detailed off to paint the outside of the bridge in the afternoon, during make and mend time. For some reason, I wasn't my usual cheerful self, and with the hot sun beating down, I wasn't enjoying the task one little bit. The lads wandered about, occasionally exchanging a few words of cheer, when a 'bumboat' came alongside, flogging so-called cherry brandy, which I quite enjoyed imbibing onshore. I was working away up the ladder, sweating like a chief stoker on watch, when an 'oppo' invited me to drink from his bottle which, in my present mood, was fatal. I shinned down the ladder, had a good swig, and had just climbed up again when another voice invited me to indulge, so down I came again. This time I had just had a fair old swig, when someone else invited me to join in, so I thought, 'Bugger the painting' and stayed where I was on the deck! One drink led to six others and so on and eventually I simply passed out and the lads dragged, me uncomplaining, along the port passage and deposited me on my bunk, where I commenced to sleep the sleep of the young and innocent and of course, the pissed! I could have survived that but, unfortunately, Smolger decided to indulge too and his bunk was next to mine. He suffered from asthma, which the nightly smoke screen laid down had not improved, and whilst lying on his bunk had a frightening attack, at which the lads panicked and called the Skipper, who entered the messdeck and saw yours truly lying in a drunken stupor on his bunk when he should, by now, have been on watch on the upper deck!

That was it, and next day, when fairly sober, I was charged with, 'endangering His Majesty's ship, L.C.I. 297 and the lives of her ship's company, by being drunk on duty'. I truly expected to be shot at dawn, every day for a week!

The Skipper was not empowered to deal with so heinous an offence, so the case was forwarded to the Flotilla Officer who was! Smolger was there too and he was sentenced to fourteen days' number elevens and my sentence was reduced because the FO felt that I had been led astray by the older man! Smolger's comments on that decision were unprintable! Next day, as the L.C.Is were loading with troops, a Regulating Petty Officer appeared, as if by magic, for no-one had even seen one since leaving UK Dressed in battledress, boots and gaiters, with our matelots cap perched on top of the head and carrying a Lee Enfield rifle, we were marched ashore, on to the jetty where, in front of curious Ities and disbelieving soldiers, we were ordered to hold the rifle above the head bend the knees and hop along the jetty!

This was no skylark and I was beginning to get annoyed, when Smolger collapsed with an asthma attack and the R.P.O. marched over to where he lay, gasping for breath and started prodding him with the toe of his boot and hurling obscenities at his prostrate body. I seized my rifle by the barrel and advanced towards the R.P.O. with it held high, about to whack him over the bonce with it! Fortunately for him and for me, of course, Paddy and Mick were already advancing to Smolger's aid, and approaching from behind, Mick seized the rifle and Paddy wrapped his long arms around me. The 'pongoes' were by now, cheering wildly and shouting, 'Good old Jack, hit the bastard', but it was all over and we never did complete the punishment, for that night we sailed for Anzio!

# CHAPTER FIFTEEN

*Anzio Annie.*

The unopposed landings had taken place before our arrival and we carried members of the Guard's Brigade as part of the build up in our forces in preparation for the expected onslaught by the German Army, who had been taken completely by surprise!

Two British L.C.Is were to act as communications headquarters for the port, one lying alongside the mole, connected by landline to the Army H.Q. ashore, the other to anchor in the bay and signal, by light, to approaching ships, with instructions for berthing or unloading on arrival. We carried out those tasks, week about, one week alongside, then a week in the bay which, particularly at night, was a hazardous place to be in.

The upturned hull of the British cruiser, *HMS Spartan*, sunk off the beach-head, could be seen, the anti-fouling paint looking as clean and smart as the day it was applied, not so long ago. What a tragic loss of a brand new ship and her gallant men, on what was probably the first operation for both ship and men! R.I.P.

There was no peace for anyone at Anzio, night or day, from the incessant shelling and bombing by the German guns and aircraft, but the task of building up men and materials in the beach-head went on just the same. A mass of men and material poured in day and night, as the German forces attacked with unequalled ferocity and our own men defended with determined stubbornness.

At night, there were threats from E-boats, and German one-man torpedoes, one of which landed up on the beach near the front line, after being launched too soon, running out of oxygen and thinking that he was behind his own lines. Tough!

A constant stream of L.C.Is tied up alongside, quickly unloaded, and were on their way again, happy to leave this dangerous place, in one piece! Negro labour battalions unloaded the LSTs and transports, with the ubiquitous DUKW., which had revolutionised close supply facilities, first at Sicily and thereafter, when adequate ports were not available and the inherent cheerfulness of the coloured soldiers had to be seen to be believed. They were great!

Some smaller vessels came alongside the mole, ahead of 297 and our piratical instincts came to the fore when it was seen that FOOD was being unloaded. Every time the Air Raid red warning sounded, the Negro stevedores took refuge inside the hollow wall, which ran the whole length of the seaward side of our position and when they did so, we nipped out smartly and 'whipped' anything that might be of use to us, but we always took full cases and never items from a case, so that people in forward positions did not receive supplies with some of the contents missing.

On one occasion, Paddy was hanging about the upper deck, filling his lungs with fresh air after a spell down below, when the warning sounded and the working party scattered to cover. Paddy seized his chance and, darting along the jetty, hoisted a fifty-six pound bag of flour on to his brawny shoulders and staggered back towards 297 when, as he neared the latter, being bent double with the weighty bag, a pair of legs, clad in olive green trousers appeared before his eyes. It was an American officer, obviously without a sense of humour who growled in his best 'John Wayne' manner, 'Put it back, or I shoot!' Paddy at first thought it was one of the lads skylarking and carried on walking (staggering) on his way, but the officer unbuttoned his holster and prepared to carry out his threat! Knowing how 'Gung Ho' some of the younger Yanks were, Paddy finally believed him and deciding that being shot dead for a bag of flour was definitely not the way to go. He shuffled back and dumped the bag where he had 'lifted' it from. The Yank made no further comment and returned to the comparative safety of inside the wall!

In the R.N., when Action Stations sounded, every-one on board had a particular 'station' to which they closed up, which meant that if the ship were hit, at least the ship's company were spread out and not concentrated in one place.

An American L.C.I., ahead of 297, learnt this vital lesson the hard way. On hearing the red warning, they fell in on deck, port side to the jetty, in what we described as a 'big heap'. An aircraft flew swiftly overhead, dropped a single bomb, which hit the jetty alongside them and the carnage was indescribable! The screams of wounded and dying men rent the air as, sick at heart, we fired in our fury at the wave of aircraft that sped toward us!

Days later, it was our turn, but fortunately our casualties were slight in comparison. Waves of bombers, escorted by fighters, swooped overhead en masse and we fired as they approached 297. I had just emptied a magazine and as Paddy, my No. 2, stretched forward and slammed a new magazine in place, there was an almighty bang, a red mist before my eyes and a giant hand slammed me back across the gun and against the gun shield. I didn't know what day it was and could see only a red haze in front of me but, according to onlookers, I jumped up and started firing overhead.

Paddy lay on the deck clutching his stomach and moaning whilst 'chef', my No. 3, was scrabbling on the deck trying to force his head, and I suppose, finally, his body, through the gap between the steps around the gun-pit!

The attack ended and several crewmen ran forr'd to our assistance. Paddy was conveyed to hospital by Army ambulance but, to our surprise and pleasure, returned on board next morning looking pale, but determined. 'Bugger that', he said, 'It's worse in the hospital than it is here. Bloody shells whistling overhead all bloody night'. 'Chef' managed to remove several splinters from his 'bonce' and seemed none the worse for his 'crawling' experience, though he was heard to mutter that he did wish he had a smaller head!

General Alexander visited the beach-head, looking calm and relaxed, as he passed across 297 on his way to the jetty and a tour of the lines, showing himself to the gallant men who had fought so well under his overall command.

When our turn came to take on the harbour job, we doubled the watch to two men on duty at night, but should there have been a determined attack from seaward, I doubt if we would have stood much chance!

We soon became used to the daily, routine shelling, etc. and when visiting L.C.I.s. came alongside, discharged their troops and quickly fled back to the safety of Naples, we assumed an attitude of careless bravado until they had departed and not one man among us wouldn't have rather have been departing with them!

The infamous 'Anzio Annie' blasted away at the harbour area and a voice over the radio drew our attention to L.S.T.s. leaving the beach-head for the return run and seeking to demoralise the remaining troops, spoke of our American allies leaving us in the lurch by running away back to Naples. It did seem uncanny, though, for whenever this lie was broadcast, sure enough, an American L.S.T. would be leaving harbour!

The most popular form of propaganda was in the form of 'porno' leaflets scattered by the enemy guns or dropped by aircraft over the harbour or beach-head area, in which a drawing of a well-formed white girl was relaxing on the bed, while a big, coloured American GI, gazing at her naked charms approvingly, was pulling on his trousers with a happy smile on his face! These leaflets provided a welcome relief from the horrors of war and were much sought after!

## Cairo.

After a month at Anzio, our relief arrived and we left quickly, sailing directly for Port Said and eventually, five days' leave in Cairo, which was choc-a-bloc with Allied Servicemen.

The sheer luxury of a full night's sleep in a bed, with freshly ironed sheets, with no night watches, alone, made our stay a complete success, but the food and feeling of being in civilisation again, even for a short while, was the icing on the cake!

The dirty, dusty, noisy streets of Cairo thronging with a great unwashed mob of beggars, con artists, 'smallie boys', shoe-shine boys, who would rub a dirty rag over one shiny boot, while his 'oppo', complete with shoe-shine gear, waited further along the pavement to redress the balance, were just a few features of this teeming city!

The con of the woman, 'baby' in arms, falling under the gharry horse and the resultant hubbub, all carefully crafted to make the embarrassed passenger pay compensation, which the driver and the woman shared, was a trick as old as the hills, but still they tried to work it, hoping to get at least one 'sucker' to pay up!

We visited several nightclubs, had more than a few beers from time to time and endured the sight of several, fat, tired old belly dancers, hawking their wares, but after enjoying the dark, voluptuous beauties of Italy, they seemed blowsy and unattractive by comparison and I didn't fancy any of them!

We posed for photographs in front of the Sphinx of Giza, the face of which looked more battered, in reality, than in any picture I had ever seen and we crawled through a long, dark, dusty passage into the tomb of Tutankhamen in the Valley of the Kings, west of Thebes, where the first stone, blocking the entrance, was removed on 25<sup>th</sup>

November 1922, allowing Lord Caenarvon and Howard Carter a first glimpse of the incredible treasures buried therein!

We gazed, in awe, at the many treasures exhibited in the Cairo Museum and such was the sheer range of minutiae on show there, that it was easy to imagine how life in Egypt under the Pharaohs had been lived.

Our short stay was soon ended and we returned to Port Said and sailed once more for Naples where, on entering the fleet canteen, for a few jugs, our 'oppo's from the flotilla gazed on us as if they had seen a ghost!

'Well, you might look more pleased to see us', we quipped and they replied in awed voices, 'We thought you were dead'.

Apparently, two nights after we left Anzio, a bomb fell between the jetty and the L.C.I. that had relieved us and it capsized, trapping the crew below. As we had sailed directly for Port Said and didn't return to our old haunts in Naples, the rest of the flotilla assumed we had been sunk! No wonder they had looked a bit 'off colour' when we strolled in, as full of life as ever!

We celebrated our return from 'the dead' in fine style and leaving the club, much later, I staggered off down the Via Roma, with a giant gladioli stuffed into the front of my bush shirt singing 'Mammy', at the top of my voice! Happy days!

# CHAPTER SIXTEEN

*Malta and Stella.*

During our nocturnal activities around the Yugoslav coast, we had suffered some underwater damage and as the only slipway capable of handling L.C.Is was in Malta, that was our next port of call, so after calling farewell to the flotilla oppos, off we sailed, with a great feeling of anticipation, for Malta was renowned as a fantastic run-ashore for the Navy and so it proved to be!

After dirty, stinking Cairo, Malta was indeed a revelation and we entered the famous harbour, cruised along Sliema Creek, and secured at the slipway on Manoel Island, ready to be winched up clear of the water to enable repairs to be carried out to the hull.

Right opposite, on Sliema front, was the Carolina bar and that was always our first point of call ashore, where we always received a great welcome from mine host, the proprietor, the delectable Polly!

I always loved Malta and the Maltese people, for they were clean and cheerful with a sunny disposition and would do anything to ensure that 'Jolly Jack' ashore had a good time, without the rip-offs common to so many other ports of call in the Med. Most matelots spent their time ashore sampling the numerous delights of Strait Street, known affectionately to generations of matelots as the 'Gut' where, if you couldn't enjoy a fantastic run ashore, you would have to be either a miserable bastard, or just plain dead!

From top to bottom, on both sides, it was bars all the way, with loud music, each bar trying to outdo the others and hordes of pretty, 'friendly' girls, who indulged in a myriad of tricks to entertain and amaze you. The fun went on all night and every night and never seemed to slacken in its intensity.

I had the obligatory couple of runs there, but settled on Sliema, not as bulging with matelots as Valetta, with a more residential atmosphere and later I felt sure I had made the right decision.

On Sunday mornings it was customary, in the Navy, to hold church services on board but, as small ships didn't carry even a C. of E. padre, when in harbour, Roman Catholics were allowed to proceed ashore to the nearest RC church. Some 'unbelievers' said that it was the only reason they were Catholics anyway and resented them being accorded the privilege, but I personally thought, 'good luck' to them!

Mick was a Catholic, so on Sunday mornings in Malta he was off ashore to the Jesus of Nazareth church on Sliema front, near the ferry station. Beer was still in short supply, and in some bars, it was customary to buy a bottle of wine before the owner would be up front with the beer. The wine, Ambique, was a dreadful shock to the palate and left a brownish, red deposit around the lips after sampling it, which was disgusting!

Due to my generous nature, I usually rounded up the bill to the next pound or two, depending how sloshed I was and this paid off, for the boss of the Cairo Bar, near the J. of N. church, recognised this inherent generosity and made it known that, simply because he liked the 'cut of my jib', I could have all the beer I wanted, providing it was hidden, out of sight, under the table.

The scene was set! Mick proceeded ashore to the Cairo Bar, got the beers in and when I arrived there was a plentiful supply, ready and waiting. It was clean and comfortable there, with a friendly staff who made us weary matelots very welcome and it was in that special place that I met the girl I next fell head over heels in love with!

Her name was Stella and she certainly was the brightest star in my firmament for the duration of my visits to Malta!

Long, dark, lustrous hair, a lovely face, with full, rich lips and eyes that shattered my lonely heart every time I gazed adoringly into their mysterious depths. Her body was slim and firm, with a well-shaped, generous bust. To me, she was like some dark, unattainable goddess and I loved her with all my aching, crumbling heart.

Stella was quietly spoken and, as the daughter of a Maltese mother and an English father, rather better educated than most of the women I had known and spoke English like a native of that country. In short, I thought she was perfection personified and, during our long relationship, she never once led me to believe otherwise.

She was also warm and passionate and gave freely to me what was a special brand of love! We sat quietly, talking and enjoying the peaceful, cosy atmosphere of the bar and when she was ready to leave, we hailed a passing gharry and travelled just around the corner to her upstairs flat, where we hurriedly ripped off our restricting clothing and made wild, passionate love on the cool, mosaic-tiled floor. Hours later, we bathed together in a spacious bath and she rubbed down my slim, tanned body, with a soft, sweet-smelling towel and cooked a delicious, light meal, which we ate together, with eyes only for one another.

We lay together naked on the bed and explored the warm, secret places of our firm, young bodies and made love again and again until, at last, we slept entwined in a gentle embrace!

I awoke about 0630, my usual time and gazed down on her lovely face, even more beautiful in repose and slipped quietly from the bed and to the bathroom for a quick washdown, before returning on board.

Carrying my boots, I crept soundlessly across the floor, trying not to awaken Stella from her well-earned rest, when, just as I neared the door, she opened her lovely eyes and whispered softly, 'Just once more, Sam, before you go''. Off came the bush shirt and shorts and within seconds we were wrapped in love's sweet embrace!

On leaving, my quivering legs wobbled at the bottom stair from her flat and when I approached the gangway to return on board, the QM. looked at me with concern on his features and muttered the immortal words, 'My God, Sam, have you had an accident?'

Malta, for me, was a very tiring place in which to be and once again, as at Algiers, I was desperately unhappy to leave, but the war progressed and 297 had been out of the fray for too long, so our sailing orders arrived and we were off once more, back to Pozzuoli, and away from my beloved. We spent a last, emotional evening locked in each other's arms and then, tearfully, we parted, swearing our eternal love!

We arrived in Pozzuoli, and the place was a hive of activity with preparation for yet another landing but, of course, no-one knew what the target was as usual. We loaded up with soldiers, tough-looking French Assault troops with small mountain guns and mules, so we gathered that this one would be a little different to the others and it certainly was!

It was to be the first major operation organised by Combined Operations alone and they were responsible for the planning, supply and success of it. Rear-Admiral Thomas Troubridge in the headquarters ship, Royal Scotsman, was in command and two China River gunboats were there to provide support. Because of the shallow nature of the bay in the middle of the southern coastline of the island, the Golfo di Campo, the gunboats and LSTs were the largest ships to be involved in what was to be named as Operation Brassard, and the 'expert' opinion expected that opposition would 'not be heavy'.

So much for experts!

# CHAPTER SEVENTEEN

*Able was I, ere I saw Elba.*
The flotilla sailed for Porto Vecchio, Corsica, where a vast armada of landing craft was assembled. The usual single German aircraft flew over the harbour and just about every craft assembled there let fly and there were so many projectiles in the air at one time, that I reckon an armour-plated bird could have walked on them!

Next morning we were away and heading for Elba, where the great Napoleon had been imprisoned. It was supposed to be lightly defended, as enemy troop movements had been observed of late. What the observers forgot to notice, was that these movements were into the island and not out, a vital difference, methinks!

Fortunately, perhaps, we knew nothing of this and in we sailed, full ahead, in the second wave of L.C.I.s. As we approached the beach, all was quiet and it looked as though the experts were right in their assumptions, but as the leading craft neared the beach, all hell broke loose and it was obvious that the enemy was lying in wait for us. Mortars, shells from heavy guns and German eighty-eights, fell right on the beach area. To compound the misfortune, there was an unreported shallow beach, right where the landing was to take place and the first wave grounded on it, a sitting target for the enemy guns who, it was subsequently discovered, had been carrying out ranging exercises on that very beach.

The skipper yelled, 'open fire', as we slewed to starboard and made at full speed for the secondary beach, previously agreed upon for such an eventuality and I aimed at the nearest gun-flashes, away from the actual beach area and opened fire with a will!

Shells were falling all around us, but the exhilaration was terrific and we were really hyped up at that moment! We reached the target beach without damage and 'tucked in' under the protective shelter of the overhanging cliffs, where our superb French troops landed on the rocks, and carrying mountain guns, spare barrels, ammunition and countless other appendages, swarmed up the cliff face like a horde of giant spiders and soon vanished from sight over the top!

Enemy long range guns were dropping shells astern as we lay there and phosphorus bombs fell amongst the Senegalese troops, who ran around the decks screaming, tearing at the sticky mixture with their bare hands and finally, jumping into the sea, where many of them perished.

Film star Douglas Fairbanks Jr, whom I had met a lifetime ago on board *HMS Rodney*, now a Lieutenant-Commander USN., was in command of a 'noises off' operation, on the other side of the island, in which his task was, in a craft fitted with loud-speakers, to create a diversion by playing recordings which simulated a landing there and thus create confusion amongst the enemy and, hopefully, cause them to divide their forces to meet both threats.

Smoke-laying craft, fitted with huge propellers, cruised up and down in an attempt to screen our activities from the Germans, but sometimes acid used in the mixture to make smoke caused more discomfort to our own forces in the vicinity than it did to our opponents.

Eventually, some sort of order prevailed and things quieted down a bit, so we hauled off the beach and set sail for Pozzuoli and sanctuary!

# CHAPTER EIGHTEEN

*Dust & dance.*
During our time in that port, where the legendary film actress,
Sophia Loren, spent her childhood (I often wished I had known her)
we were present when no less than three volcanoes erupted at the
same time. Stromboli did so, continuously and molten lava could be
seen clearly at night, running down to the sea, but such eruptions were
rarely seen from the peaks of Etna and Vesuvius, so it was quite an
auspicious occasion when this happened during our spell in Pozzuoli.

Ships in the harbour were covered with a grey dust, which settled
and found its way into nooks and crannies, everywhere and we kept
all doors and hatches tightly closed until, thankfully, the situation
returned to normal!

We spent one hilarious night in a small fishing village called Bhia,
a few miles from Pozzuoli, when an L.C.I., one of our flotilla, was in
collision with another vessel at sea, just off the coast, and was
seriously damaged. It was, in fact impaled on the bigger ship's bows,
which was steaming slowly, in circles, to prevent a sudden rush of
water which would, no doubt, have capsized the L.C.I.

We left Pozzuoli in a rush and steamed, at full speed, to the scene,
where we carried out a difficult manoeuvre to come alongside the
landing craft, lash her securely to our bollards, and with men standing
by with fire axes to sever the ropes, should the stricken vessel threaten
to capsize and take us with her, signalled the big ship that we were
ready for her to move astern and free herself from the smaller vessel.
Slowly astern she went and as she did so, the L.C.I. heeled over at a
dangerous angle, but the ropes held fast and we moved slowly off
towards the nearest point on the coast, the aforementioned Bhia,
where on arrival, we beached both craft, bows on and secured for the
night. On strolling ashore, we found the locals were very pleased to
meet us, their liberators from both Mussolini and the hated Germans.
We repaired to a simple hall with whitewashed inner walls and there
they lashed us up to a seemingly inexhaustible supply of Italian
champagne, which we downed with some pleasure. A one-legged,
blind fiddler was guided into the hall and the fun really began! He
fiddled away furiously and, as the evening wore on, became more and

more unsteady on his single 'pin'. Such was the enthusiasm of his playing that he kept overbalancing and we would simply haul him to his feet and off he would go again! I think it was the high peak of his whole life and he was determined to enjoy the moment, which he surely did.

Later, quite naturally, the 'champers' worked on everybody, matelots and locals alike and the smooching started. I took this buxom wench outside against the wall, for the traditional knee-trembler and if you think that I took advantage of a simple fisher lass, then think again, for she was well versed in the delicious art of love and within seconds, our clothes were off and 'Ole Nobby' was driving in and out, just like the fiddler's elbow, inside the hall!

We crept back aboard in the early hours of the morning, and when we awoke with a splitting headache and a completely shattered spine, the lads who remained on board remarked what a boring place it was and we, of course, agreed with them!

# CHAPTER NINETEEN

*Symi and the goats.*
We returned to Pozzuoli with the survivors and their kit and prepared to spend a restful few days recuperating after our gallant rescue mission, but it was not to be, for we were detailed for another 'mystery mission' and we sailed for the island of Symi, about which not one of us had a clue, concerning its whereabouts and what its importance was to the war effort, but we soon found out!

'297' secured alongside the jetty in a beautiful natural harbour, which was surrounded by tier upon tier of tall houses, which had been built into the hillside. Legend had it that this tiny island, one of the Dodecanese chain of islands, was the place where Prometheus, the Titan who stole the gift of fire from heaven, came down to earth, and as a punishment for this dastardly act, Zeus turned him into a monkey (simia) and, to this day, no self-respecting inhabitant, will allow himself, to be called a Simian, but a Symiot!

Symi was about a four hour ferry ride from Rhodes which, at that time, was still occupied by the Germans, who also held a ring of small islands, which were lightly garrisoned by their troops. Set up in caves on Symi, there was a sophisticated, intelligence gathering unit and night raids were frequently carried out on these islands for intelligence gathering, and with the added purpose of harassing their German garrisons.

An ancient German aircraft flew, daily, to Rhodes and it was allowed by the Allies to do so, simply because the mail that it carried from the Homeland was the best source of information available to our intelligence services about conditions and the state of mind of the people back in Germany!

Our job was to carry raiding groups to the islands, land them there and carry them and their prisoners if any, back to Symi, where prisoners would be interrogated and the captured mail sifted through in search of any item of information which could be of use to the Allied cause. This we did, creeping out of harbour at night, sometimes lying close inshore, while the raiding group slipped ashore on their dangerous mission, or beaching in some small, secluded cove and awaiting the return of the raiders.

During our time there, we carried a wide assortment of troops, including Long Range Desert Group, SAS., Indian and Greek forces and it was a privilege to be associated with such men, who cheerfully and confidently went about their work with many a ready quip and not a word of complaint about the difficulties of their nocturnal tasks!

On one particular occasion, we carried a party of Greeks, members of the Sacred Heart Regiment, who wore the emblem of a red heart upon their breast and were considered to be a crack, elite body of fighting men.

We had beached just before dawn and they went ashore with dry feet, which was a change for them and there was no opposition at the landing point. We stood by cocked guns, ready for any emergency, when suddenly small-arms fire broke out close by, followed by the crump of grenades exploding, then silence!

As we stood tensely there, to our guns, an astonishing sight greeted us! Down a winding path, came four stark-naked men carrying a Greek soldier on a stretcher, who we could already see was badly wounded. The tiny cortege came up the ramp and carefully laid the stretcher on the deck, and then departed, back from where they had come!

The wounded man of the Sacred Heart Regiment lay quietly there without a sound, although he was fully conscious and only murmured once, when someone, thinking he would be more comfortable, attempted to move him into the shade, for the sun was, by now, blazing hot. He indicated that he wanted to remain where he was and we looked on, feeling helpless.

I brought some water in a bowl, and with a damp cloth attempted to cool his brow and he smiled in obvious gratitude. I sat close to him and held his hand, at which he opened his eyes and just looked at me. He was too badly wounded for us to do anything except try to make him as comfortable as possible and we winched off the beach and proceeded at full speed to an attendant destroyer which lay just off-shore where, with great tenderness, he was lifted on board, at which point he was still alive!

We returned to the beach and the rest of the raiding party were there waiting for us, with several prisoners under guard, one a German officer, immaculately dressed. The Greeks were concerned about the condition of their wounded comrade and we assured them that he was now in good hands.

They told us what had happened and how he was wounded and the reason for the German stretcher-bearers being starkers. Apparently, the Greeks had called upon the German garrison to surrender and after some discussion, they agreed to do so. They raised their hands in surrender and came forward towards the Greeks and as they did so, one at the back threw a grenade, which exploded close to the man accepting their surrender and, as it later proved, mortally wounded him!

Accordingly, the Germans were ordered to strip naked, which they did and were then detailed to carry the wounded man back to the landing craft.

What happened to the man who threw the grenade, no-one would say, but I would proffer an opinion that he reached his ultimate destination well before the young man he had so cruelly wounded.

On a lighter note, we were invited by the locals to take part in a goat hunt and we readily agreed to do so. Off we went up the steep slopes, topped up with beer and ouzo, making as much noise as was possible, hoping to drive the goats which ranged freely on the hills, into the clutches of the waiting locals which, to their delight and ours, they did do and the hunt was declared a success.

Along the jetty was a small covered platform jutting over the water, with a large hole in the base of it and we had wondered what was its purpose, thinking, perhaps, that it was some kind of handy toilet when taken short while working in the vicinity, but now we were to see a demonstration of its official use.

The unfortunate goat was dragged inside, its head manoeuvred over the hole and then chopped off with one swift blow! This went on until the captured goats were disposed of and in honour of our participation, we were presented with the pick of the bunch, which they butchered for us (we pleaded lack of experience in such matters) and we duly cooked and ate it, finding the taste to be similar to that of a piece of ancient mutton and quite stringy to boot!

There was a NAAFI canteen manager on the island, whose store was down by the harbour and he, apparently, took a great fancy to me, which was a great source of amusement to the lads. He used to bring quantities of booze, cigarettes and other 'goodies' on board and this, of course, proved extremely useful. For the first time since leaving the States, we had everything we could desire but, after a while, the funny bit wore off and I found his constant attentions embarrassing although, to be honest, he never made a move to collect payment of any kind, fortunately!

# CHAPTER TWENTY

*Bar and boxes.*

Two of the caiques that roamed these waters, seemingly at will, manned by a villainous-looking crew of tough matelots, visited Symi and they spent an evening at the bar on the waterfront. Their boat was anchored in the harbour and so that they could proceed back and forth between boat and shore, without tying anyone up on board, they secured their dinghy to an endless line so they simply heaved on the line and went ashore, or back on board, at will and the dinghy was always available company and we'd had a great sing-song and general skylark, when it was time for them to return on board. They all trooped out to the jetty and piled in a big heap into the tiny dinghy, all standing up. Singing and shouting, someone heaved on the rope and the dinghy started to move. It was so overcrowded that it gradually began to sink lower and lower in the water until, at one point, just the heads were above the surface. Suddenly, it sank and everyone vanished from sight for a few seconds, then they surfaced, a laughing, cheering crowd struggling in the clear, crystal water.

It was far and away the biggest laugh we had had for years and the locals enjoyed it too, as they laughingly related to us next day. Next morning, when we surfaced, bleary-eyed and hungover, we looked across the harbour to their billet, but it was empty and they had departed, as silently as they had arrived and we never saw them again!

One day, poking around on shore, Mick, Paddy and I came across the local cemetery, which was very small, even for such a tiny island and we saw a number of huge wooden boxes, which had a tarry appearance, obviously blackened with age, ranged along the longest wall of the rectangular shaped plot. Being naturally curious, we decided to investigate the mysterious boxes and looking carefully around (we didn't want to upset the locals) we lifted the lid and looked inside.

They were filled with human bones of all shapes and sizes and we dropped the lid back in place quickly! The mystery of the small cemetery was explained! Apparently, when a person died, they were placed in a coffin, as is usual, and carried to the cemetery, where the lid was removed and the coffin 'lined up', length-wise, with the grave. Whilst the mourners prayed, the body was tossed in to the grave and if it landed on its back, all was well and the ceremony proceeded, but if the body landed face down, it was hauled out again and the process repeated for a maximum of three attempts. If it still landed face down, then the corpse was adjudged to be in possession of a sinful secret and a special service of cleansing and absolution had to be carried out before the body could be finally buried. After three years, the bones were removed from the grave and stowed tidily in the box for posterity!

On such a small, rocky island, land was at such a premium that the islanders had originated the perfect practical solution!

# CHAPTER TWENTY-ONE

*Stripped!*
We drank beer and ouzo and picked delicately at octopus, grilled on the embers and sprinkled with lemon and parsley. Seafood was obviously cheap and plentiful and was usually consumed, accompanied by sips of ouzo, in an atmosphere of friendly banter and comradeship. The islanders used to supply the world's markets with fine sponges, which they retrieved from the seabed locally, but when artificial sponges were brought into use, their markets virtually collapsed.

We carried on with the night raids and experienced, first hand, exactly what the locals thought of the Germans, who had occupied the islands in a see-saw struggle with the British. It was quite common, when dawn broke, after a raid on a small, German-held island, to see the naked bodies of enemy soldiers bobbing about in the sea, stripped of every article of clothing, boots and all, by the locals, who displayed a ferocious hatred of their former would-be masters!

There were no roads on Symi, just a mule track that lead from the harbour area, known as Yalou, over the mountains to the Monastery of Panormitis and the only means of transport was on the back of a donkey or on foot.

Our task in Symi was complete and German garrisons on the hotchpotch of small islands around Rhodes had been eliminated, so it was time to say 'goodbye' and move on, so we prepared for sea and said our farewells. This time, for a change, I wasn't broken-hearted at the thought but, by the look of him, the canteen manager was!

Ah! The pangs and pains of unrequited love!

We had enjoyed our stay there, for the locals were some of the friendliest encountered anywhere on our long and extensive travels around the Med, but there was one rumour I must deny, even at this late stage. I did not, at any time, have an affair with the Mayor's daughter and to the old shipmate who, fairly recently, sent me a postcard recalling it, I have just one thing to say, 'Not guilty, your honour, it's a clear case of mistaken identity!' We sailed off into the hot sun with the surface of the sea like a sheet of glass, wondering what new adventure lay before us!

# CHAPTER TWENTY-TWO

*Adonis the virgin.*

Pozzuoli once again, our old stamping ground, but this time the talk was all of a great landing in the South of France which was being planned, and which seemed to be of general knowledge around Naples but we dismissed that thought for the moment and concentrated on having a good time with old friends in the town.

In every ship's company, there are always some men who, for one reason or another, don't join in the usual runs ashore, the wenching and the drinking, etc, and spend their spare time writing home to mother or girlfriend, and to outward appearances, they seem to be very lonely. There was one lad, in particular, who always hovered on the fringes of any conversation, listening to our yarns of runs ashore and acts of daring-do with the fair sex, and one day, in an effort to draw him into the circle, Paddy addressed him directly and asked if he had ever made love to a woman! He blushed shyly and replied that he hadn't and furthermore, wouldn't know what to do!

Now this was a challenge the lads just could not pass up and we accordingly 'laid on' a date with a gorgeous girl, who was a friend of mine and lived in a house nearby. The lad, Jim, was over six feet tall, with fair curly hair and the looks of a Greek Adonis and we could foresee no problems after he had been given a short course of instruction into the finer arts of love.

On the chosen night arranged with the girl in advance, we trooped ashore in a state of great excitement! Jim looked quite pale and apprehensive, but we jollied him along and he even raised a weak smile once! We had a couple of drinks just to oil the wheels, as they say, and then repaired to the house of the chosen one where, on arrival and after fixing her dark, hungry eyes on this fine specimen of manhood, she led him off into her inner sanctum.

Above the door was a glass skylight and we grabbed chairs, stools or anything to stand on and watched operations eagerly!

I believe that in the heat of the supreme moment, he forgot our careful instructions and when she stripped him off and he stood before her, like a Zanzibar bloodhound, all 'dick and ribs' and as she gazed, in awe, at his mighty member, he panicked, for despite all her eager, experienced coaching, his drooping manhood hung down, as limp as last week's lettuce!

The girl's frustration was terrible to behold, as she rubbed it, kissed it and moved her body over it, to no avail! Suddenly, she gave an almighty shriek, walloped him on the chin and half-dragged, pushed and kicked him from the room! This had gone too far and as we consoled him with promises of more specialist training, ready for next time, I, as the youngest and fittest, was elected to restore the girl's usual good humour, which, stripping off, strictly in the line of duty of course, I did to the best of my ability.

One other lad on the messdeck was a really serious person, and read enormous books on all kinds of remote subjects when he wasn't writing letters to his beloved, to whom he had become engaged, after a mutual, 'swearing eternal love to each other' session, before leaving England. He made out an allotment of money from his meagre pay and for nearly two-and-a-half years stayed on board, volunteered to do other people's duties if they wanted to go ashore and were on duty watch and was, generally, a useful bloke to have around but when, later on, we were told that we would be going home soon and he wrote off, full of joy, at the prospect of seeing his beloved again, she wrote back saying that she had married some time ago and that she loved another! She still continued to draw the money, of course!

That was a difficult time for him, but he bore his sad loss bravely, didn't go off the rails, to try to make up for lost time and earned the respect of us all for his quiet dignity of bearing throughout his miserable ordeal.

In my long spell in the Royal Navy, especially during eight years service in the Regulating Branch, I came across many such cases, and through that experience formed the considered opinion, that most men were happy in the Service until they fell into the clutches of predatory females, who were abundant and caused much unhappiness to us 'simple sailormen'. It was my misfortune during that time to be involved with a number of suicides and suicide attempts and in every case, a woman was at the root of it and the best policy, in my book, was to love 'em and leave 'em, for there were always plenty more where they came from!

# CHAPTER TWENTY-THREE

*Smokey.*

During our stay in Pozzuoli, the differences between standards of living of the Americans and our own Services became very apparent and we constantly gave thanks to them, both for their innate generosity and for the quality of the stores, both food and clothing, supplied by them! Everyone serving there during Christmas 1944 remembers the bitter cold of an Italian winter, when deep snow covered the land and we struggled, desperately to get and stay warm. Americans on nearby landing craft fitted us up with warm, lined parkas and other items of warm clothing.

One day, a chef, from an American L.C.I., complete with tall, immaculate, white hat, wandered on board and asked to see our chef, whom we had incidentally 'lost' some time ago as the result of an accident and whose duties where carried out by a volunteer crew member. Apparently, the Yank wanted to swap some thirty frozen chickens for a quantity of our corned beef, as his crew were fed up with eating chicken and wanted a change of diet! No problem, for apart from the chickens we had swapped for packets of used tea, with a sprinkling of 'new' tea leaves on the top, we had been unable to indulge in that delicacy and just couldn't wait to get at them.

Many times when we loaded American troops on board, prior to an operation, American Red Cross girls would arrive before sailing and distribute a whole carton of cigarettes of various brands to each man, and pass among the men with trays of paperback books, from which they chose whatever was of interest to them.

Our lads had a choice all right! Take it or leave it! That was the only choice and I'm sure that many of the 'manky' old fags, with brown age spots on the sides, were packed in the 'C' rations at the time of the first 'Great War' but, we were only serving our country, anyway!

Our girl in the town was happy again, after her experience with 'Adonis', and when the cold spell came, in an effort to please me, she lit a wood fire in the ancient fireplace of her home. I don't know when this momentous event had last occurred, but the chimney definitely didn't like it a bit, for it smoked like a bastard and after a love session during which we could hardly see one another, in that hot, smoke-filled room and when I rejoined my comrades outside, they all laughed like a drain, for my face was black and streaked with white lines of perspiration!

# CHAPTER TWENTY-FOUR

*South of France.*

Ships of all shapes and sizes, including battleships and aircraft carriers from both Britain and America, plus some large French warships, were gathering off Naples and troops poured into the port and into Pozzuoli, where the main body of L.C.Is were assembled.

This apparently was to be, in the main, a Franco-American Armies' show and the prospect didn't exactly fill me with confidence, mainly because rumours of impending landings on the coastline of Southern France had been circulating for ages and I couldn't imagine the Germans sitting there quietly with a bunch of flowers waiting for us to land, but I worried needlessly, for when we ground ashore at St. Raphael, the giant pillbox dominating the beach was silent and empty and no hail of withering fire greeted us!

It was most uncanny, for after all, this was the Allies' first major landing on this side of fortress Europe and we expected the Germans to defend it tenaciously.

The Army, tough-looking French troops, walked comfortably ashore and I still couldn't believe that there could be no opposition and that a sudden blast of gunfire wouldn't shatter the uncanny silence!

We three forr'd guns crew were standing there talking, looking uneasily around, when suddenly a single bullet whistled past our heads. We dived behind the gunshield and took cover, but a 'gung ho' sub-lieutenant R.N. (yes, they had finally infiltrated Combined Ops, unfortunately) grabbed a rifle and started blazing away towards the woods into which the soldiers had disappeared. Shouts and cries came from our own men, for him to 'knock it off' and, finally, the 'dickhead' got the message and put the rifle down, before someone shot him!

It was like a summer picnic, the quietest operation of them all, and now perhaps we could go home, the lads could return to 'civvy street' and I could start on the long, lonely ten years that I still had to serve in the Royal Navy, a prospect that filled me with no joy at all. But that lay in the distant future and we had to return to Pozzuoli and carry on doing what had to be done, until the time came for us to start on the long journey home!

Pozzuoli was quiet now, for the bustle and clamour of war had moved on and it was just another backwater that had served its purpose, then reverted to its former state of slumber.

We still held the food parties daily and the abundance of small, hungry children was as before, but their channel of support had shrunk with the departure of so many servicemen and we thought, who will feed them when we have gone and will their new, democratic government care for its children any better than the Fascists had done?

I am not a religious person in any way, but it does seem to me, a simple, old sailorman, that the riches and treasures of the Roman Catholic Church would be better employed in feeding and caring for its innocent children, than being seen on display in its mighty churches and cathedrals!

# CHAPTER TWENTY-FIVE

*Love bonus.*

At last, winter was over and the weather started to warm-up a bit, which was not too soon, for I was 'browned off' with steaming sex, in hot, smoky rooms, and beginning to resemble a well-cured kipper!

Our sailing orders arrived and we were bound for Malta, the land of the divine Stella and I could hardly wait to see my beloved again!

Cruising along under clear blue skies, without fear of some rotten bastard trying his level best to ruin our day with bomb or torpedo, made for relaxed, easy sailing, and that trip was just like a Mediterranean cruise, with the vital difference, that we were being paid to do it by His Gracious Majesty, the King!

We tied up in Sliema Creek and, after a quick shower (one of the great benefits of American-built craft, along with the coffee percolators) I sped ashore at a rate of knots to the Cairo bar and on entering and gazing anxiously around its cool, cosy interior, I saw her sitting quietly in a corner, where I had first seen her, watching, with dark, beautiful eyes, the world pass by.

She looked, disbelieving, looked again, and we were suddenly back in each other's arms, after what seemed a lifetime apart and without ado, left the club, reached Stella's flat and throwing off our clothes, were soon locked in intense, passionate love! Hours later, we awoke, hungry (for food, this time) and after our ritual bath together, sat down to a delicious meal, then with the 'sap' swiftly rising, went back to bed and drifted off, in a magical world of sensuous love-making!

We both knew, in our hearts, that our time together was short and I would probably return to England and home soon, so we spent as much time together as we could. We held hands and kissed in the protective darkness of the cinema, though afterwards, neither knew or cared what the film was about. We strolled, hand in hand, along Sliema front, or sat on the warm rocks, with feet dangling in the clear, blue sea and wished that our idyll could last forever, but sadly, of course, it could not and sailing orders arrived and 297 was off once more!

More sad, tearful goodbyes and I reflected afterwards that this had been the pattern of my life to date! Hello and goodbye and it was likely to be so for some time yet!

# CHAPTER TWENTY-SIX

*Peace and home.*

Our destination this time was Port Said, a return visit, but now the war was practically over in Europe and we hoped, with the Suez Canal being so close, that our final destination was not to be the Far East!

We were in dry dock, a weld, right forr'd, having split when, one day, suddenly sirens sounded all over the port and people were shouting, singing and dancing like madmen, and the war was over in Europe!

Immediately, all the bars shut in the town and once ashore we finished up drinking 'Stella' beer in a barber's shop, but we celebrated the occasion in fine style and later, when we were all awarded two days' leave we continued the celebrations throughout that two day period.

Next, to our great relief, the signal arrived for us to sail home, so our fears of a long trip to the Far East were proved to be groundless. Off we sailed, this time in the right direction and after a series of overnight visits to places we had visited on the way out so long ago, when the forces of our country were poised for the great breakthrough into the soft underbelly of Europe, we were home!

We left L.C.I. 297, which had been our only home for two-and-a half years and in which we had sailed many thousands of miles across the seas, secured to a buoy in a quiet, Scottish loch and travelled by lorry and train to Glasgow and thence to Westcliffe-On-Sea, near Southend in Essex. By a lucky coincidence, the train stopped at signals, at the back of my 'local' pub, the Ship and Shovel, where I had stood on the table and made a stirring speech, praising the good people of Dagenham a life-time ago!

There were two small boys playing at the side of the track and on seeing our brown faces, they came over and asked where we were going? I told them Westcliffe and asked if they knew Mrs. Garrod and they said that they did and she lived at No 6, Canonsleigh Road, near them!

In my 'small' bag, I had a pound tin of cigarette tobacco for Dad, which I had purchased in America, a bottle of neat pussers' rum for yours truly and some 'goodies' for Mum and the girls and I gave the boys ten 'bob' each to deliver them to Mrs. Garrod and to tell her that Sam would soon be home, which they readily agreed to do!

There was great excitement in the 'Garrod' household that night, but it was two days later when we were finally free to go home,  In that time, many good people had been very busy and as I turned the corner, the street was a mass of flags and banners with a message which made all that had passed seem worthwhile!

### 'WELCOME HOME, SAM!'

# EPILOGUE

I took part in and very much enjoyed the round of parties which greeted not only my return, but the return of many other young men in the vicinity of Canonsleigh Road, Dagenham, at that time and when the war with Japan ended too, and a second round of celebrations started, we began to look forward to a New World, where fear, hunger, poverty and war would be eradicated but, alas, it was not to be, and when one looks at the world around us today, can we be forgiven for thinking was it all worthwhile?

I have enjoyed a full and varied life, hoping never to have been evil, though on occasion wicked, perhaps, but one incident still fills me with deep regret, even after so many years have passed by, and that was when I made love to the charming and innocent wife of my best friend, Tom Pepper, an incident for which I was totally to blame and which caused the break-up of our friendship, after all the tough times we had endured together!

I can only fall back on an old Navy adage, although that is still no excuse for what I did!

Sex will draw a man further than gunpowder can blow him!